THE
GEEKY
BARTENDER
DRINKS

THE
GEEKY
BARTENDER

REAL-LIFE RECIPES FOR FANTASY COCKTAILS

DRINKS

CASSANDRA REEDER, THE GEEKY CHEF

Race Point
PUBLISHING

Inspiring | Educating | Creating | Entertaining

Brimming with creative inspiration, how-to projects, and useful information to enrich your everyday life, Quarto Knows is a favorite destination for those pursuing their interests and passions. Visit our site and dig deeper with our books into your area of interest: Quarto Creates, Quarto Cooks, Quarto Homes, Quarto Lives, Quarto Drives, Quarto Explores, Quarto Gifts, or Quarto Kids.

Text © 2015, 2017, and 2018 by Cassandra Reeder
Photography © 2015, 2017, and 2018 by Quarto Publishing Group USA Inc. (pp. 12, 18, 21, 25, and 26 © Shutterstock)

This edition published in 2020 by Race Point Publishing, an imprint of The Quarto Group,
142 West 36th Street, 4th Floor, New York, NY 10018, USA
T (212) 779-4972 F (212) 779-6058 www.QuartoKnows.com

First published in 2018 as *The Geeky Chef Drinks* and includes recipes from *The Geeky Chef Cookbook* (2015) and *The Geeky Chef Strikes Back* (2017) by Race Point Publishing, an imprint of The Quarto Group, 142 West 36th Street, 4th Floor, New York, NY 10018.

Race Point titles are also available at discount for retail, wholesale, promotional and bulk purchase. For details, contact the Special Sales Manager by email at specialsales@quarto.com or by mail at The Quarto Group, Attn: Special Sales Manager, 100 Cummings Center Suite, 265D, Beverly, MA 01915, USA.

10 9 8 7 6 5 4 3 2

ISBN: 978-1-63106-709-9

Library of Congress Control Number: 2019957597

Publisher: Rage Kindelsperger
Creative Director: Laura Drew
Editorial Project Manager: Leeann Moreau
Managing Editor: Cara Donaldson
Senior Editor: Erin Canning
Cover and Interior Design: Amelia LeBarron
Photography: Bill Milne
Illustration (p. 8): Denis Caron

Printed in China

CONTENTS

77
CULTY COCKTAILS

97
LITERARY LIBATIONS

111
DYSTOPIAN POTIONS

121
COMEDIC CONCOCTIONS

137
NONALCOHOLIC BEVERAGES

Crafting

INTRODUCTION

Since, well, birth, but more publicly since I started *The Geeky Chef* in 2008, my passion project has been making recipes for fictional or unusual foods from books, TV, movies, and games. I don't know if it's the tendency of us writers to, well, let's say, have a disposition toward alcoholism, but a whole lot of these foods tend to be alcoholic beverages. Enough to fill a whole book of their own. This book, actually.

The bad news is, I'm not a mixologist. I'm not Guinan or Quark. I'm definitely not Sam Malone. I'm not even Tom Cruise, though I am his height and much less likely to sue you. That being said, I have had some practice at drink-making over the years as The Geeky Chef. I actually learned a lot just making this book. So, the good news is: If I can learn to make a decent cocktail, you absolutely can, too! These are cocktails for geeky laymen by a geeky lay . . . man. The other good news is, I have some friends (I know, it's a miracle I have friends at all!) who are also bartenders, and they gave me some great cocktail wisdom, a burden I now pass on to you, Padawan.

I will try to keep things as simple as possible, but I do recommend these five things:

1. **Get a cocktail shaker.** I cannot stress this one enough: The use of a cocktail shaker can improve a cocktail by approximately 1,000 percent! Mixing glasses can be sort of improvised, but the mystical effects of a cocktail shaker can't be understated. There's a reason James Bond likes his martinis shaken . . .

2. **Embrace the bitters.** Outside of the bartending world, unsavvy folks like you and me may not understand the power and appeal of bitters. I'm here to tell you, they are like the seasoning of drinks, the final incantation that makes the potion fully effective. Don't be afraid of the "bitter" in the name; most of them aren't even particularly bitter. They're called bitters because the essence of their flavor is distilled from their ingredients, sort of like The Force being distilled into a sprinkle-ready bottle.

3. **Use simple syrups.** This is the best way to sweeten a cocktail, period. Adding a touch of sweetness and flavor, they easily dissolve into liquids and can vastly improve any cocktail.

4. **Adjust ratios to your liking!** If you like a stiff drink, bump up the alcohol or reduce the mixers. If you like a mellower drink, lower the alcohol amounts and/or increase the non-alcoholic ingredients. If you like a sweeter drink, just increase the amount of syrup, soda, or juice. Despite what some may have you believe, crafting cocktails is not an objective science. You won't have Professor Snape slapping your hand if you don't add exactly three drops of dragon blood while stirring counterclockwise for five-and-a-half turns, I promise.

5. **Buy like the smarty-pants nerd you are.** Unlike my previous books, I couldn't completely avoid expensive or unusual ingredients. Alcohol is just *not cheap*. I did avoid naming specific brands whenever possible, but sometimes I had to cite specific products for their unique color, flavor, or effects. My advice is, buy the stuff you like in bulk at warehouse clubs, and if you're not sure you're going to like it, buy the little mini bottles. Those little guys usually run to $1 to $4 for about 50 ml of liquid—and they make great potion bottles later!

LIQUID MEASUREMENT CONVERSION

½ fl oz	1 tablespoon	15 ml
¾ fl oz	1½ tablespoons	22 ml
1 fl oz	2 tablespoons	30 ml
1½ fl oz	3 tablespoons	45 ml
2 fl oz	¼ cup	60 ml
3 fl oz	6 tablespoons	90 ml
4 fl oz	½ cup	120 ml
6 fl oz	¾ cup	180 ml
8 fl oz	1 cup	240 ml
16 fl oz	2 cups/1 pint	475 ml

SIMPLE SYRUPS

It's all in the name. Simple syrups are just that: simple. Simple to make, simple to use, and once you get the hang of them, you can easily make your own magical concoctions. Lavender honey syrup? Yes! Blueberry cinnamon syrup? Go for it! Here are some of my favorites to get you started.

— STERILIZING TIP —

It's best to store simple syrups in airtight, sterilized storage containers (a thick glass bottle or jar with a lid works best). The easiest way to do this is to use the dishwasher's high temperature setting. No dishwasher? Here are some instructions on how to sterilize heat-resistant glassware:

1. Place the glass container(s) right side up in a canner or a deep pot with a rack at the bottom.
2. Fill the canner or pot with water until it is 1 inch (2.5 cm) above the container(s).
3. Bring the water to a boil over medium-high heat and continue to boil for approximately 10 minutes.
4. Reduce the heat and keep the container(s) in the hot water until you're ready to fill with syrup.
5. Remove from the hot water carefully with protective gloves and/or tongs.

CLASSIC SIMPLE SYRUP

1 cup (200 g) granulated sugar
1 cup (240 ml) water

1. In a saucepan, combine the sugar and water.
2. Bring to a boil and cook over a medium heat, stirring regularly, until the sugar has dissolved, about 3–5 minutes.
3. Allow to cool before storing in an airtight storage container.

FRUIT SYRUPS

There are basically two ways to make fruit syrups: you can begin with either fresh fruit or fruit juice.

You can substitute different kinds of fruit in the blueberry syrup for a different flavor, although berries work best. I like raspberries and strawberries myself. Likewise, you can substitute any kind of juice in the grenadine recipe, including cherry or pineapple.

— **STORAGE TIP** —

Add 1 tablespoon (15 ml) of vodka to the syrups after they are prepared to make them last longer in storage. They usually keep for about a month in the refrigerator.

GRENADINE

Most of us are familiar with grenadine as the red, artificially flavored, candy-like cherry syrup you get at diners and soda shops, but originally, grenadine was made using fresh pomegranate. I'm not saying you have it make it from scratch, but I *will* say you *should*, because your taste buds will throw you a party.

1 cup (240 ml) pomegranate juice (preferably one without added sugar)
¾ cup (150 g) granulated sugar
1 teaspoon fresh lemon juice
2–3 drops orange flower water

1. Mix the pomegranate juice and sugar in a small saucepan and cook over a medium-low heat, stirring, until the sugar has completely dissolved.
2. Reduce the heat to low and continue to cook, stirring occasionally, until the mixture has thickened, about 20 minutes. Remove from the heat and stir in the lemon juice and orange flower water.
3. Let cool to around room temperature before storing in a sterilized, airtight container.

BERRY SYRUP

1 cup (100 g) frozen or fresh blueberries, blackberries, strawberries, or raspberries
1 cup (240 ml) water
½ cup (100 g) granulated sugar
1 teaspoon lemon zest

1. Add all the ingredients to a saucepan and bring the liquid to a boil.
2. Reduce the heat to low and simmer for 15 minutes.
3. While still hot, pour mixture through a mesh strainer into a sterilized, airtight, heat-resistant storage container.
4. Let the syrup cool to around room temperature before using or capping the container.

HERBAL SYRUPS

I love to use herbal syrups in my baking and cooking, but especially in my drinking. The great thing is, the method is pretty much always the same, though some herbs or spices may need additional "steeping" time if you want a strong flavor.

LAVENDER SYRUP

3 tablespoons dried lavender buds (culinary grade) or 3 lavender tea bags
1 cup (240 ml) water
1½ cups (300 g) granulated sugar

1. Add the lavender to the water in a saucepan and bring to a boil, then stir in the sugar and cook until it's fully dissolved, 3–5 minutes, stirring occasionally.
2. Reduce the heat to low and simmer for about 15 minutes.
3. Remove from the heat and allow to cool and steep for 45 minutes.
4. Strain the syrup into a sterilized, airtight container.

GINGER SYRUP

¾ cup (75 g) peeled and sliced fresh ginger
1 cup (240 ml) water
1½ cups (300 g) granulated sugar

1. Add the ginger to the water in a saucepan and bring to a boil, then stir in the sugar and cook until it's fully dissolved, stirring occasionally.
2. Reduce the heat to low and simmer for about 15 minutes.
3. Remove from the heat and allow to cool to around room temperature, as the ginger infuses the syrup.
4. Strain the syrup into a sterilized, airtight container.

CINNAMON SYRUP

5 cinnamon sticks
1 cup (240 ml) water
1 cup (200 g) granulated sugar

1. Add the cinnamon sticks to the water in a saucepan and bring to a boil, then stir in the sugar and cook until it's fully dissolved, stirring occasionally.
2. Reduce the heat to low and simmer for about 15 minutes.
3. Remove from the heat and allow to cool and steep for 45 minutes.
4. Strain the syrup into a sterilized, airtight container.

OTHER SYRUPS

HONEY SYRUP

¾ cup (180 ml) water
¾ cup (255 g) honey

1. Add the water and honey to a saucepan.
2. Heat over a medium-high heat, stirring occasionally, until the honey dissolves into the water, but don't boil.
3. Let cool to around room temperature before storing the syrup in a sterilized, airtight container.

BROWN SUGAR SYRUP

1 cup (240 ml) water
1½ cups (340 g) dark brown sugar
1 teaspoon vanilla extract

1. Add the water and brown sugar to a saucepan and bring to a boil, stirring regularly.

2. Reduce the heat to low and continue stirring until all the sugar has dissolved.

3. Remove from the heat and stir in the vanilla.

4. Let cool to room temperature before storing the syrup in a sterilized, airtight container.

SPICED MAPLE SYRUP

½ cup (170 g) real maple syrup
½ cup (120 ml) water
2 whole allspice
2 cinnamon sticks
2 whole cloves
2 star anise

1. Add the maple syrup, water, and all the spices to a small saucepan.

2. Bring to a boil and then turn off the heat.

3. Cover the pan and let the syrup cool and steep for 45 minutes.

4. Strain the syrup into a sterilized airtight container.

SPECIAL EFFECTS

We're making magical and high-tech drinks here, and sometimes they need to look more, well, magical and high-tech. How or whether to garnish is totally up to you, but here are some impressive ways to decorate a drink. With special effects, you can choose just one, or use multiple effects for a very impressive-looking drink!

RIMMING THE GLASS

SUGARED/SALTED RIM

This is a classic. Any type of sugar or salt can be used, but as a rule you don't want to pick one that's super fine or super coarse. You can also purchase cocktail rimming sugars and salts, which have been crafted with the intention of being used to rim cocktail glasses and come in a variety of flavors and colors.

HOW TO RIM A GLASS

1. Add sugar or salt to a shallow dish.
2. Moisten the rim of the serving glass. (Water works fine in most cases.)
3. Dip the glass into the salt or sugar.
4. If you want more sugar or salt on the rim, slightly twist the glass.

HOW TO COLOR SUGAR OR SALT

1. Put ¼ cup (50 g) of sugar or salt in a small, resealable plastic bag.
2. Add a drop of food coloring.
3. Seal the plastic bag and shake for a few seconds.
4. If the color is too light, add another drop of food coloring and repeat step

SPARKLY RIM

If you want to add some glitz and glitter, this is a great way to bedazzle your cocktail. Edible glittercan be purchased in the baking section of most grocery stores, at a baking store, or online. I used the Wilton brand, but CK Products are also popular.

Edible glitter (any color)
A little light corn syrup or honey

1. Place the edible glitter in a shallow bowl or dish that the top of your glass will fit into.

2. Use a pastry brush (or your finger if you don't mind getting sticky) to apply the corn syrup or honey around the rim of the glass. You could also squeeze a ring of corn syrup or honey onto a dish and dip the glass into it.

3. Dip the sticky rim of the glass into the edible glitter or sugar to coat. *Voilà!* You have an impressive-looking drink with little to no effort.

— **TIP** —

For a thicker coat, twist the glass.

CANDY RIM

1 cup (200 g) granulated sugar
½ cup (120 ml) light corn syrup
½ cup (120 ml) water
Candy thermometer
Food coloring (any color)

1. Combine the sugar, syrup, and water in a heavybottomed pot over medium-high heat, and pop in the candy thermometer. Don't stir until the liquid reaches 300°F (150°C).

2. Once heated to 300°F (150°C), remove the thermometer and stir in the food coloring, making sure the color is evenly mixed in.

3. Dip the heatproof serving glass into the mixture while it's still hot, then turn it upright, being careful not to let any syrup get on you. The syrup will drip down the glass and then harden for a drippy effect.

— TIP —

It can be a bit difficult to remove the candy from the glass after it hardens, but soaking it in soapy hot water for a half hour or so should loosen it.

THE SKEWER

The skewer is a quick, easy way to add flair to any drink. All you have to do is skewer stuff onto a toothpick and drop it into the drink. You can also get fancy and cut shapes out of fruits (e.g., strawberry hearts, pineapple stars), or purchase themed skewers for occasions like Halloween or Cinco de Mayo.

— TIP —

Make sure to skewer stuff with flavors or colors that complement the cocktail. You don't want to add a pickle skewer to a Shirley Temple. Or maybe you do!

ICE EFFECTS

Altering the appearance of ice is another easy way to add flair to a drink.

SHAPE

For most cocktails, ice cubes or spheres are best for taste because their melt rate is consistent. However, some more concentrated drinks, like the Mint Julep, benefit from faster-melting crushed or cracked ice. You can also use fun molds to make ice that jibes with the drink's theme. There are all kinds out there: stars, leaves, skulls, etc. I've even seen Tardis, Starfleet, and R2-D2 molds!

COLOR

An easy way to add color or flavor to any drink is to make ice cubes with fruit juice or food coloring. If the recipe calls for orange juice, go ahead and freeze some orange juice in ice trays and add it to the drink. Food coloring can be added to regular water and frozen if you just want a color effect. These look especially cool in clear or light-colored drinks.

GARNISH

Freezing fruit, herbs, edible flowers, or any other edible garnish is another easy and impressive way to add a nice visual element to any drink. For this method, you need to boil distilled water, then let it cool before pouring the water into an ice mold and adding the garnish. Boiling the water first allows you to make an ice cube that is more transparent and less cloudy.

THE SPIRAL CITRUS PEEL

Citrus fruits are probably the most common drink garnishes. Most of the time, all you have to do is cut out a slice and drop it in the drink, but you can also cut them into shapes. My favorite citrus garnish is a peel twist. A lot of folks will tell you that you need to peel the citrus fruit a certain way to get the right shape, but that's just not true.

A small citrus fruit (e.g., lemon, tangerine, lime)
A sharp knife

1. Take your fruit and cut out a round slice from near the center. The slice should be about ¼ inch (6mm) thick.

2. Cut out the center of the slice, removing as much pith (i.e., the white stuff on the inside of the rind) as you can without cutting through the peel itself.

3. Once the pulp and most of the pith is removed, use the knife to cut the circular peel so that it is one long strip.

4. Use your fingers to roll the peel strip into as tight a spiral as you can without breaking it.

— TIP —

For tighter twists, drop the peel into a glass of ice water immediately after creating the spiral.

THE SHIMMER EFFECT

Edible "luster dust" can be used to add sparkle and shimmer to frostings, gum paste, and fondant. Luckily for us, it can be used in beverages, too! This shimmery liqueur will add some magic to any cocktail or potion without changing the flavor too much. You can make your own sparkly concoctions by combining any clear liquor you plan to use in your cocktail with any flavor of simple syrup and any color of luster dust!

1 cup (240 ml) clear liquor, such as vodka, white rum, or gin
½ cup (170 ml) Classic Simple Syrup (page 11)
Pinch or 2 edible luster dust

1. In a small mixing bowl, stir the liquor and simple syrup together with a whisk until the syrup has completely dissolved, about 3 minutes.
2. Gradually whisk in the luster dust.
3. Use a funnel to pour the mixture into a glass bottle. Store in the refrigerator for up to 2 weeks.
4. Swirl the bottle to activate the luster dust before using it in a cocktail.

— **TIP** —

You can find edible luster dust in the baking section near the cake decorations in some grocery stores, in any baking store, and online. Amazon carries a few brands like Wilton, CK Products, and Bakell at reasonable prices.

THE MIST EFFECT

Dry ice adds a bit of mystery to any special brew.

Supplies

Dry ice	Flat-head screwdriver
Towel or other thick fabric	(or something that can be used as a chisel)
Safety goggles or other eye protection (recommended)	Thick rubber gloves (recommended)
Hammer	Tongs
	Serving vessel(s)

1. Carefully place the dry ice on the towel and sort of bunch up the towel around it, making sure you do not touch the ice directly. Use the towel to pick up the ice then flip it over onto your work surface.

2. Put on goggles or other eye protection. Use the hammer and screwdriver like a chisel to carefully break up the dry ice into smaller cubes. The size of the cubes depends on whether you are using the ice in the serving glasses directly or in a larger container (like a punch bowl).

3. Use tongs to drop a cube into your serving vessel(s) right before you pour in your drink of choice.

FOR YOUR SAFETY

1. Go full mad scientist and equip yourself with safety goggles or other eye protection and thick rubber gloves.

2. NEVER CONSUME OR DIRECTLY TOUCH DRY ICE, even after it has been added to the cocktail. It can be very dangerous and even cause frostbite. Make sure everyone consuming your beverages knows this.

— TIP —

Purchase the dry ice a couple hours before planned use, at most. Standard freezers are not cold enough to maintain dry ice. It will melt.

PLAYING WITH FIRE

1. Fire and drinking are not the best of friends, so make sure you're sober when attempting to light a drink. You do NOT want to end up like VADER WITHOUT THE SUIT!!!

2. NEVER drink a cocktail that is currently lit. Wait for the flame to die or snuff it out yourself.

3. DO NOT attempt to blow out the flame. This only spreads the fire.

4. ALWAYS make sure the glass, your hands, the counter, the lighter, and anything else you don't want to set on fire have no alcohol on them. In fact, it's best to remove anything flammable from your prep area.

5. DO NOT use a thin cup or glass; it could shatter from the heat.

6. DO NOT use a plastic cup or a plastic straw if lighting a drink.

7. Sometimes the fire is hard to see, especially if you're in an area with a lot of light. If you've lit the drink and you don't see flames, try turning down the lights. ALWAYS assume the drink is lit and treat it with care.

THE FLAMING FLOAT

Supplies
A cocktail
Thick, heatproof glass
Any 151-proof liquor
Tablespoon
Utility lighter
Fire extinguisher

1. Prepare your cocktail and pour it into the glass. Make sure that there is 1–2 inches (2.5–5 cm) of space below the rim.

2. Once your cocktail is properly prepared, pour some of the high-proof liquor into the tablespoon. Gently spoon the liquor over the drink so it creates a separate top layer.

3. Use the utility lighter to light the alcohol on top of the drink. Stand back and admire, take pictures, etc.

CAUTION

Make sure the fire is extinguished before putting the cup near your face. Flames usually burn out in a minute or so.

THE CITRUS FLAME

This is a garnish that's more about flavor than style—at least after the trick is done. The act of flaming the citrus is pretty stylish, though, so you'll probably get some "oohs" and "ahhs."

Supplies
Paring knife
Fresh citrus fruit (usually an orange)
Utility lighter or match
A cocktail

1. With the paring knife, cut out a 2–3-inch (5–7-cm) piece of citrus peel, trying not to get too much pith.

2. With your lighter or match, hold the flame a few inches (7 cm) above the drink.

3. Squeeze the peel over the flame, with the outside of the peel facing down. You'll want to squeeze hard enough to extract enough oil from the peel.

4. Drop the peel into the drink as a garnish.

CAUTION

Be prepared for a burst of flame when the oil from the peel makes contact with the fire.

OTHERWORLDLY
INTOXICANTS

WHITE-GOLD TOWER

SERVES 1

Skyrim, I just can't quit you. Every *Elder Scrolls* game is a triumph, but *Skyrim* is the only one I've picked up again four times in seven years and done something completely new every single time. Some things just get better with time. Like *Skyrim*. And alcohol. *Skyrim* has its fair share of alcoholic drinks for your Dragonborn to find or purchase; the most intriguing of these are Talen-Jei's cocktails at The Bee and Barb in Riften. The White-Gold Tower is described as a layered drink containing blended mead, heavy cream, and lavender. It is then topped with Dragon's Tongue, which is a kind of flower in *Skyrim*. This recipe blends two kinds of mead, lavender syrup, and bitters, and tops it off with heavy cream and an edible flower.

INGREDIENTS

2 fl oz (60 ml) dry mead
2 fl oz (60 ml) Cyser mead
½ fl oz/1 tablespoon (15 ml)
  whiskey (optional)
4–6 dashes of lavender bitters
1 teaspoon Lavender Syrup
  (page 14)
Ice cubes
1 fl oz (30 ml) heavy cream

1. In a cocktail shaker, combine both meads, the whiskey (if using), bitters, syrup, and ice cubes. Shake well.

2. Pour the mead mixture into your serving glass.

3. Pour one-third of the heavy cream out of the carton and set aside (you can pour it back in later). Shake the heavy cream carton vigorously for about 30 seconds.

4. Get a spoon and hold it upside down above the mead in the glass, tilted slightly downward. Slowly pour the heavy cream onto the back of the spoon so it indirectly spills over into the glass on top of the mead. It's important not to do this too quickly if you want a layered effect.

SUGGESTED SERVING VESSEL

Highball glass

SUGGESTED GARNISH

Edible flower (nasturtium blossoms, orchids, and viola flowers look the most like Dragon's Tongue)

VELVET LECHANCE

SERVES 1

Velvet LeChance, also sold at The Bee and Barb, is described as having blackberries, honey, spiced wine, and a touch of *nightshade*. I went for a pretty literal interpretation of the drink because it already sounds pretty amazing. I know the nightshade they are referring to is the deadly flower, but, luckily for us, the term nightshade could refer to potatoes, paprika, and eggplant, which are all in the nightshade family (although perhaps not the best cocktail ingredients . . .). I thought the best nightshade to add to this drink was cayenne pepper, to give it a bite.

INGREDIENTS

5 blackberries
1–2 teaspoons Honey Syrup
(page 15)
2 fl oz (60 ml) crème de mûre
(blackberry liqueur)
4 fl oz (120 ml) bottled spiced/
mulled wine (or see Mulled
Wine recipe on page 108)
Tiny pinch cayenne pepper

1. In the serving cup, gently muddle the blackberries with the syrup.

2. Pour in the Crème de Mûre, top with the wine, and stir to combine.

3. Top with a tiny pinch of cayenne pepper to serve.

SUGGESTED GARNISH/EFFECT

The Skewer (page 19) with blackberries

The Mist Effect (page 23)

TIP

New to muddling? Here's how: Press the berries into the bottom of the glass with a "muddler" or wooden spoon, while twisting your wrist, for 10–15 seconds.

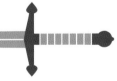

THE YELLOW FAIRY

SERVES 1

Microsoft Game Studio's *Fable II* is a game with an unprecedented amount of choices, including drinking yourself into a stupor, purchasing property, and getting married (probably in that order and probably all in one night). The alcoholic drinks in *Fable II* have amusing punny names, granted skill points, and are a great gift for your angry and neglected spouse(s). The Yellow Fairy, a play on "The Green Fairy" (aka absinthe), is one of two five-star drinks in the base game, meaning it is a quality item. And it seemed to lend itself best to a cocktail interpretation. The in-game description is that it tastes like marshmallows and may cause liver damage. This is a very strong, bright yellow cocktail with a hint of marshmallow flavor.

INGREDIENTS

1½ fl oz (45 ml) whipped cream
  or vanilla vodka
1 fl oz (30 ml) overproof
  white rum
½ fl oz (15 ml) amaretto liqueur
2 fl oz (60 ml) pineapple juice
1 tablespoon (15 ml) fresh
  lemon juice
1–2 teaspoons Brown Sugar
  Syrup (page 16)
3 ice cubes

1. Add all the liquid ingredients to a cocktail shaker with the ice cubes.

2. Shake until chilled.

3. Strain into a small bottle or a glass.

SUGGESTED SERVING VESSELS

Cork bottle

Glass mug

SUGGESTED GARNISHES

Dollop of Marshmallow Fluff

The Spiral Citrus Peel (page 21) with lemon

NOBLE PURSUIT

SERVES 2-3

Breath of the Wild was everything *Zelda* fans wanted and more. It boasted a giant world with multiple unique regions. In the desert region, Link happens upon a Gerudo named Pokki, inconveniently languishing on top of the Misae Suma Shrine's door-opening pedestal. Pokki tells Link that she's dying of thirst and that only a specific drink, the "Noble Pursuit" from The Noble Canteen in Gerudo Town, will save her. Thus begins the quest for "The Perfect Drink," which involves a Gerudo disguise, underage bar-going, and a giant ice cube. For this drink I used two real-world counterparts to in-game ingredients that have a cool or heat-resistant effect: hydromelons (watermelons) and cool safflina (lavender). It really is the perfect drink.

INGREDIENTS

3 cups (450 g) cubed fresh watermelon
2 fl oz (60 ml) cold water
2 fl oz (60 ml) light rum
2 fl oz (60 ml) gin
4 teaspoons Lavender Syrup (page 14), or to taste
Juice of 1 lime
½ cup (70 g) ice cubes

1. In a blender, blend the watermelon until smooth.
2. Strain the watermelon through a fine sieve into a pitcher, discarding the pulp.
3. Add all the remaining ingredients to the pitcher and stir.
4. Pour into serving glasses.

SUGGESTED GARNISHES/EFFECTS

Ice with lavender buds (page 20)
Sprig of lavender
The Mist Effect (page 23)

VIRGINIZE

Omit the rum and gin, adding ½ cup (75 g) of chopped watermelon and 2 fl oz (60 ml) of water.

SULFURON SLAMMER

SERVES 1

Blizzard's *World of Warcraft* is the most-played MMORPG of all time. I would know, I spent most of my free time in Azeroth from 2006 to 2007. There are many alcoholic consumables in *WoW*. SO MANY. I wanted to choose drinks that had something special going, like the Sulfuron Slammer. The item description says it is an extremely potent flaming alcoholic beverage: "It'll knock your socks off . . . and then set your feet on fire." Like most alcohols in *WoW*, this one can cause blurred vision and cockiness, but it'll also literally set you on fire. Spicy, sweet, and the color of sulfur, thish drink ish . . . Hic! What was I saying?

INGREDIENTS

2 fl oz (60 ml) gold tequila
1 fl oz (30 ml) Ancho Reyes
½ fl oz (15 ml) amaretto
2 fl oz (60 ml) pineapple juice
2–3 dashes Angostura Bitters
2–3 ice cubes

1. Add all the liquid ingredients to a cocktail shaker with the ice cubes. Shake well.

2. Strain into a serving glass.

SUGGESTED GARNISH/EFFECT

Jalapeño slices

The Flaming Float (page 25)

MOONGLOW

SERVES 1

Moonglow, described as a strangely glowing alcoholic beverage, can be purchased in most of the major cities during the Lunar Festival—a celebration of the Lunar New Year by the Druids of Moonglade. The icon shows a bottle full of a pale blue phosphorescent liquid. When consumed, your character will sparkle and glow! This drink includes moonshine (because, ya know, the whole moon thing), Hpnotiq for the color, and tonic water to make it glow under a blacklight.

INGREDIENTS

¾ fl oz (22 ml) moonshine
2 fl oz (60 ml) Hpnotiq liqueur
¼ tablespoon (4 ml) fresh
   lemon juice
1 teaspoon Classic Simple
   Syrup (page 11)
3 ice cubes
3 fl oz (90 ml) tonic water

1. In a mixing glass, stir together the moonshine, Hpnotiq, lemon juice, and simple syrup, along with the ice cubes.

2. Pour the contents of the mixing glass into a serving vessel.

3. Top with tonic water and stir.

4. Turn on a blacklight.

5. Douse yourself with glitter. Or don't.

SUGGESTED SERVING VESSEL

Round cork bottle

VIRGINIZE

Omit the moonshine and replace the Hpnotiq with blue Hawaiian Punch or similar.

GROG

SERVES 2

Pretend fantasy pirates are great. Real pirates . . . well, they're less fun. Grog is the No. 1 preferred drink of pretend pirates everywhere. My personal-favorite grog is in the *Monkey Island* series, where it is bright green and eats through solid metal, which is way more useful than using carrot cake to break people out of prison. This version is inspired by the Caribbean-influenced grog of the pirate days of yore, but decidedly modernized. *Monkey Island* fans can add blue curaçao and green food coloring to make it that bright acid green.

INGREDIENTS

4–5 ice cubes
3 fl oz (90 ml) spiced rum
1 fl oz (30 ml) coconut rum
4 fl oz (120 ml) pineapple juice
3 fl oz (90 ml) orange juice
2–3 teaspoons Cinnamon Syrup
   (page 15), or to taste
Juice of 1–2 limes
Pinch sea salt
1 fl oz (30 ml) blue curaçao
   (optional)
Few drops green food coloring
   (optional)

1. In a large mixing glass, add the ice cubes and all the ingredients. Stir together.
2. Pour into the serving vessels.

SUGGESTED SERVING VESSELS

Metal mug

Goblet

SUGGESTED GARNISHES

Tiny Jolly Roger

VIRGINIZE

Omit both rums and the curaçao, and add one drop of coconut extract and extra cinnamon syrup. For the green color, add green food coloring.

MAGICAL ELIXIRS

AMOR DI INFIERNO

SERVES 1

Grimm is a fantasy police procedural that follows Nick, a homicide detective who finds out he is a descendent of a line of supernatural hunters called "Grimms." Grimms are responsible for keeping the balance between humanity and supernatural entities known as "Wesen." In the season 6 episode "Blind Love," Nick and his friends are the target of a revenge plot that involves a potion called Amor di Infierno, which, loosely translated, means "Love of Hell." Sounds lovely, right? It causes the drinker to fall madly in love with a specific person and, ultimately, become so overwhelmed with emotion that they self-destruct. This potion can only be created with the saliva (yum!) of a kind of Wesen called a cupitas, along with a piece of hair from the target love interest and any liquid carrier. Cupitas saliva appears green, so to represent it, I made a concoction of Chartreuse, pear juice, honey, and bitters. We'll just go ahead and skip the pieces of hair . . .

INGREDIENTS

1 fl oz (30 ml) Chartreuse
1 fl oz (30 ml) pear juice
1 teaspoon Honey Syrup
   (page 15)
Dash Angostura Bitters
3 ice cubes
3–4 fl oz (90–120 ml) brut
   champagne

1. First, make the Cupidita's saliva (yum . . .). In a cocktail shaker, combine the Chartreuse, pear juice, syrup, and bitters with the ice cubes. Shake well.

2. Strain into a champagne flute.

3. Top with champagne.

CHATEAU ROMANI

SERVES 2

Majora's Mask is a game that has tons of strange and fascinating side quests. My two favorites are the ones that result in Link getting some booze-milk. Described as a "vintage" milk, a serving of the stuff fully restores Link's health and boosts his magic meter, making it the most useful consumable in the game. But drinking too much just makes you a sad drunk like Gorman. It is only produced by the very special cows at Romani Ranch. Preventing their abduction by aliens is the best way to get a free bottle, and since one bottle costs a whopping 200 rupees at the Milk Bar in Clock Town, you're definitely better off saving the cows. Put on your cow mask and savor this decadent vintage milk, which is enhanced with bourbon, Irish cream liqueur, and a hint of coffee liqueur to restore your energy.

INGREDIENTS

1 cup (240 ml) whole milk
2 fl oz (60 ml) bourbon
2 fl oz (60 ml) Irish cream
   liqueur
1 fl oz (30 ml) coffee liqueur
2 small scoops vanilla
   ice cream
1 teaspoon vanilla extract
Pinch ground cinnamon
Pinch grated nutmeg

1. Blend all the ingredients in a blender.
2. Pour into a serving vessel(s).

SUGGESTED SERVING VESSEL

Glass cork bottle

SUGGESTED EFFECT

The Shimmer Effect (page 22)

VIRGINIZE

Omit the bourbon, use nonalcoholic Irish cream, and replace the coffee liqueur with 1 fl oz (30 ml) of brewed coffee.

HERO DRINK

SERVES 1–2

Final Fantasy is a series of science-fantasy RPGs developed by Square (now Squaresoft). The Hero Drink, also called Hero Cocktail, is a recurring item in the *Final Fantasy* series, first appearing in *Final Fantasy V*. Although the effects vary from game to game, it's generally a powerful stat booster. The color, whenever depicted, is always a bright Chocobo yellow. Drink this to cause 9999 damage. To your liver.

INGREDIENTS

2 fl oz (60 ml) light rum
1 fl oz (30 ml) banana schnapps
1–2 fl oz (30–60 ml) orange
   juice (pulp free)
2 fl oz (60 ml) pineapple juice
Ice cubes

1. Add all the ingredients to a cocktail shaker. Shake until cold, about 20 seconds.
2. Pour into a serving vessel(s).

SUGGESTED SERVING VESSEL

Small glass bottle

SUGGESTED EFFECT

The Sparkly Rim (page 18) in yellow

VIRGINIZE

Replace the rum with 2 fl oz (60 ml) of white grape juice and a squeeze of fresh lemon juice. Replace the banana schnapps with a couple drops of banana extract.

MIRUVOR

SERVES 1

The Lord of the Rings by J. R .R. Tolkien is the quintessential high-fantasy series. One thing Tolkien is known for is his extensive world-building. Ever the craftsmen, the Elves of this series make some great things: bread, swords, tree houses . . . One of the more memorable Elven gifts given to the fellowship was Miruvor. Also known as the nectar of the Valar, it was said to be made from Yavanna's flowers and thought to include honey. Clear in color, with warming properties, Miruvor helped the fellowship survive the journey through the treacherous Misty Mountains. Become "Lord of the Drinks" with this warm, floral, and invigorating beverage.

INGREDIENTS

3 fl oz (90 ml) lightly brewed and hot white tea

1½ fl oz (45 ml) elderflower liqueur

1½ fl oz (45 ml) gin (Plymouth or London Dry)

2–3 teaspoons Honey Syrup (page 15), or to taste

1 teaspoon orange blossom water

1. Pour the tea into a serving vessel.

2. Stir in all the remaining ingredients.

SUGGESTED SERVING VESSELS

Glass bottle

Crystal goblet

VIRGINIZE

Omit the gin, add another 1 fl oz (30 ml) of white tea, and replace the elderflower liqueur with 1 tablespoon (15 ml) of either elderflower syrup or Lavender Syrup (page 14).

RED POTION

SERVES 1

Red potions have been a staple in video games for decades, appearing in popular titles like *The Legend of Zelda*, *World of Warcraft*, *Terraria*, and many, many more. Red-colored potions, more ubiquitously called "health potions" or "healing potions," usually restore a character's health or vitality, making them some of the most used and most common potions in many games. This recipe has some health benefits from the cranberry juice and ginger syrup. It seems counterintuitive to add alcohol to a health drink, but, hey, sometimes a little liquid courage doesn't hurt!

INGREDIENTS

1½ fl oz (45 ml) silver tequila
1 fl oz (30 ml) Campari
½ fl oz (15 ml) sweet vermouth
1 fl oz (30 ml) cran-raspberry
    juice
2–3 ice cubes
2 fl oz (60 ml) chilled
    soda water

1. Add all the ingredients except the soda water to a cocktail shaker with the ice cubes. Shake until chilled, about 20 seconds.
2. Pour the contents of the cocktail shaker into a serving vessel.
3. Top with the chilled soda water.

SUGGESTED SERVING VESSEL

Glass bottle

Small cauldron

SUGGESTED GARNISHES/EFFECTS

The Skewer (page 19) with strawberries cut into heart shapes

The Shimmer Effect (page 22) in red, gold, or silver

The Mist Effect (page 23)

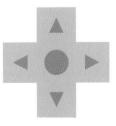

BLUE POTION

SERVES 1

Like red potions, blue potions are an RPG staple. Blue potions generally restore the player's magic points, or mana, (although occasionally it improves stamina or other stats). Since most of us don't have mana points to restore, I thought electrolytes and potassium might work. This cocktail has a nice tropical-citrus flavor, and with a bit of coconut water it will definitely refresh you . . . if not your mana.

INGREDIENTS

1 fl oz (30 ml) white rum
1 fl oz (30 ml) coconut rum
¾ fl oz (22 ml) blue curaçao
3 fl oz (30 ml) sparkling
    coconut water
1 fl oz (30 ml) fresh lime juice
1 fl oz (30 ml) Classic Simple
    Syrup (page 11), or to taste
2–3 ice cubes
2–3 fl oz (60–90 ml) chilled
    lemon-lime soda

1. In a mixing glass, combine both rums, blue curaçao, coconut water, lime juice, simple syrup, and ice cubes. Stir.

2. Pour into a serving vessel.

3. Top with the lemon-lime soda.

SUGGESTED SERVING VESSELS

Potion bottle

Small cauldron

SUGGESTED EFFECTS

The Shimmer Effect (page 22) in blue or silver

The Mist Effect (page 23)

GREEN POTION

SERVES 1

In most games where they appear, the green potions restore stamina, although there are some outliers. The magic ingredient in this delicious potion is matcha green tea powder, which will restore all your stamina—all of it!—and give you a healthy dose of nutrients to boot.

INGREDIENTS

1 tablespoon (15 ml) matcha powder

½ fl oz (15 ml) warm water

1 fl oz (30 ml) vodka

1 fl oz (30 ml) Midori

2–3 ice cubes

1 scoop lime sherbet

2–3 fl oz (60–90 ml) chilled lemon-lime soda

1. Whisk the matcha powder with the water until the powder is completely dissolved.
2. In a cocktail shaker, add the vodka, Midori, matcha mix, and ice cubes. Shake until chilled and well combined.
3. Place the scoop of sherbet in the bottom of a serving vessel.
4. Pour the contents of the cocktail shaker on top of the lime sherbet.
5. Top with the lemon-lime soda.

SUGGESTED SERVING VESSELS

Glass bottle

Small cauldron

SUGGESTED EFFECTS

The Shimmer Effect (page 22)

The Mist Effect (page 23)

GIGGLE WATER

SERVES 6

Fantastic Beasts is a prequel to the *Harry Potter* films, but it is only loosely connected to the events of the original series. It takes place in the 1920s, as magical animal rights activist Newt Scamander visits the United States to return a magical creature to its natural habitat. Giggle Water is actually an oldtimey American term for champagne, though you don't need to be a Legilimens to know this stuff ain't just champagne! Using thoroughly American ingredients like bourbon and apple cider, this delicious shooter is as American as apple pie (kinda tastes like it too), and it will make you burst out laughing.

INGREDIENTS

3 fl oz (90 ml) bourbon
1 fl oz (30 ml) butterscotch
   Schnapps
2 fl oz (60 ml) spiced apple
   cider (nonalcoholic)
2–3 ice cubes
3 fl oz (90 ml) champagne

1. Add the bourbon, Schnapps, and cider to a mixing glass with the ice cubes. Stir.

2. Divide among shot glasses and top each shot with champagne.

3. Drink in one gulp.

4. Laugh uncontrollably.

SCI-FI
SPIRITS

RYNCOL COCKTAIL

SERVES 1

You spend a good amount of time in bars in BioWare's *Mass Effect 2* (at least I did). In a game where you can get drunk and get private dances from aliens, why would you not do exactly that? Ryncol is a Krogan liquor, and anyone who has seen a Krogan knows that it's probably not a soft beverage. The pure form of Ryncol will kill a Volus and can put a human in a coma. In the game, if Shepherd orders five drinks at the Dark Star Lounge in the Citadel, the bartender will serve them a green Ryncol Cocktail. If Shepherd drinks it, they will black out and wake up on the bathroom floor. Drink this and you may end up there yourself, possibly in a space bar in the twenty-second century.

INGREDIENTS

Ice cubes
1½ fl oz (45 ml) overproof
  white rum
1½ fl oz (45 ml) Midori
½ fl oz (15 ml) absinthe
½ fl oz (15 ml) Classic Simple
  Syrup (page 11), or to taste
1–1½ fl oz (30–45 ml) fresh
  lime juice
Drop mint extract
2–3 fl oz (60-90 ml) chilled
  lemon-lime soda

1. Fill a cocktail shaker with ice.
2. Add all the ingredients—except the soda—to the cocktail shaker and shake well.
3. Strain the drink into a serving glass.
4. Top with the lemon-lime soda.

SUGGESTED SERVING VESSELS

Cocktail glass

Lowball glass

SUGGESTED GARNISH

Sky blue rock candy

Sugar Rim (page 17) in sky blue

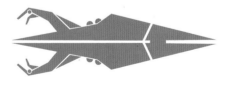

SHIMMERWINE

SERVES 2

Shimmerwine had a brief appearance in the episode "Shindig," and was sort of a throwaway line muttered by Inara when she was avoiding an uncomfortable conversation with Atherton Wing (aka "that piece of go-se"). Although it's not a huge part of the *Firefly* world—it *might* have been, *eventually*, but we'll never know because it was *cancelled*! Deep breaths, count to ten . . . the drink sounds pretty intriguing. I imagined a soft, shimmering effervescent beverage that, unlike Mal, would be right at home at fancy balls. Make it a mighty fine shindig and drink this (literally) shining cocktail while you question that buffet table.

INGREDIENTS

2 fl oz (60 ml) St-Germain
  elderflower liqueur
1 fl oz (30 ml) vodka or gin
8 fl oz (240 ml) chilled
  champagne

1. Pour the St-Germain elderflower liqueur and vodka or gin into 2 wine glasses or champagne flutes. Give it a quick stir.
2. Top off with the champagne.

SUGGESTED EFFECTS
The Sparkly Rim (page 18) in gold or champagne

The Shimmer Effect (page 22) in gold

MUDDER'S MILK

SERVES 1-2

Mudder's Milk appeared in the episode "Jaynestown." It was created in Canton, a town on a planet called Higgin's Moon. Because mudding is such strenuous work, it was prudent for the laborers to get their nutritional requirements while they got their recreational drinking on. This mysterious concoction is supposed to have all the protein, vitamins, and carbs of a turkey dinner, plus 15% alcohol. Judging from Wash's reaction, the drink is definitely supposed to be an acquired taste, but I thought it would be a nice idea to make it more palatable. **Bonus Double-Geek Fun Fact: Mudder's Milk is also a consumable in** *World of Warcraft*. **Shiny!**

INGREDIENTS

2 fl oz (60 ml) bourbon
2 fl oz (60 ml) Irish cream
   liqueur
1 cup (240 ml) whole milk
½ cup (125 g) plain Greek
   yogurt
1 frozen banana
2 tablespoons (30 g) peanut
   butter
¼ cup (20 g) oatmeal
1 tablespoon (12 g) flax seeds
1 tablespoon (10 g) chia seeds
2 teaspoons Spiced Maple
   Syrup (page 16), or to taste
Pinch ground cinnamon, or
   to taste
½ cup (70 g) crushed ice

1. Combine all the ingredients in a blender.

2. Blend until smooth.

3. Pour into a serving vessel.

4. Sing an ode to Jayne, the hero of Canton!

SUGGESTED SERVING VESSEL

Clay mug

VIRGINIZE

Omit the bourbon and use nonalcoholic Irish cream, or add more Spiced Maple Syrup (page 16).

AMBROSIA

SERVES 1

Battlestar Galactica is a 1970s sci-fi series, created by Glen A. Larson, in which humanity is threatened by robotic antagonists called Cylons. The series was beautifully reimagined in 2004 by Ronald D. Moore and David Eick. In *BSG*, Ambrosia was an expensive, strong spirit that became rare after the twelve colonies were destroyed by the Cylons. Although Ambrosia is brown in the original series, it is bright green in the rebooted series, and this is the version I'm making. So, yes, I've already made a couple versions of the green Ambrosia—all of this has happened before, and all of this will happen again, amiright? This recipe (the best one yet!) combines Navy Strength gin, melon liqueur, and citrus to make a very potent alcoholic beverage. As Gaeta says, "Ambrosia's good with a chaser." I suggest beer. Don't let the toasters get you down!

INGREDIENTS

2 fl oz (60 ml) Navy Strength gin
1½ fl oz (45 ml) melon liqueur
½ oz (15 ml) Triple Sec
1 fl oz (30 ml) fresh lime juice
1–3 dashes Angostura Bitters
Ice cubes

1. Add all the liquid ingredients into a cocktail shaker filled with ice. Shake well.

2. Strain into a serving glass.

SUGGESTED SERVING VESSELS

Cocktail glass

Champagne flute

BLOODWINE

SERVES 1

Klingons started as fairly one-dimensional antagonists in the original series and became more complex in *TNG* and *DS9*, when their culture and history were explored in depth. Bloodwine is a Klingon beverage that is so strong, non-Klingons can barely tolerate it. Although the taste of the beverage is never described, the appearance is blood red. The drink may or may not contain actual blood. In the official cookbook, Neelix states that it does, but Neelix isn't even from the Alpha quadrant, and, well, his expertise is dubious. It's more likely that it was named for its blood-like appearance, much like sangria. tlhIngan maH!

INGREDIENTS

1½ fl oz (45 ml) dry sherry
1 fl oz (30 ml) overproof
   spiced rum
½ fl oz (15 ml) cherry liqueur
2-3 teaspoons Grenadine (page
   13), or to taste
½-1 fl oz (15–30 ml) fresh
   lemon juice
2-3 dashes orange bitters
2-3 ice cubes

1. Add all the ingredients to a cocktail shaker. Shake well.
2. Strain into a serving vessel.
3. Qapla'.

SUGGESTED SERVING VESSELS

Mug

Goblet

SAMARIAN SUNSET

SERVES 1

The Samarian Sunset is an intriguing beverage. The most interesting feature is that it starts out as clear liquid and then explodes with iridescent color when subjected to vibration (flicking the glass). Its two most notable appearances are in *TNG* and *DS9*. Data makes one for Deanna Troi after losing their game of chess, as per their agreement. In *DS9*, Quark prepares the drink for his old flame Natima Lang. The special effects of this drink are impossible to replicate exactly in the twenty-first century, but using the sake-bomb technique comes pretty close!

INGREDIENTS

Ice cubes
2 fl oz (60 ml) coconut water
1 fl oz (30 ml) white rum
¾ fl oz (22 ml) shimmery white
  rum (see The Shimmer Effect
  on page 22)
½ fl oz (15 ml) pineapple juice
½ fl oz (15 ml) Grenadine
  (page 13)

1. Fill a cocktail shaker with ice and add the coconut water and the 1 fl oz (30 ml) white rum. Shake well.

2. Strain into a highball glass.

3. In a separate double shot glass, add the ¾ fl oz (22 ml) shimmery white rum, pineapple juice, and grenadine.

4. Place two kabob skewers or chopsticks about a thumb's width distance apart across the top of a highball glass. Rest the shot glass on top.

5. Using your fists, slam the table until the shot falls between the skewers and into the glass, exploding with color and eventually settling into a uniform orange. (Alternatively, you can flick the glass fairly hard until the shot drops, but unless you're an android, this might take a few tries.)

ROMULAN ALE

SERVES 1-2

Gene Roddenberry's *Star Trek* has a way of taking extremes of the human condition, sticking them in alien races, and forcing us to deal with them diplomatically. Romulans are obviously our snarky side. Their ale has been mentioned (or has appeared) in *TOS*, *TNG*, *DS9*, and some of the films. This highly intoxicating, bright blue stuff is so strong that even Klingons, who are resistant to most alcohols, suffer the aftermath. Romulan Ale has a strange legal status in the world of *Star Trek*, although if that's due to its strength or to the strained relations of the Federation with Romulans, Q only knows.

INGREDIENTS

2 fl oz (60 ml) overproof
   white rum
1 fl oz (30 ml) blue curaçao
½–1 fl oz (15–30 ml) fresh
   lemon juice
Ice cubes
3 fl oz (90 ml) chilled
   ginger beer

1. Add the rum, blue curaçao, and lemon juice to a cocktail shaker filled with ice.
2. Shake well.
3. Pour the contents of the shaker into a serving glass.
4. Top with the ginger beer.

ARDEES AKA JAWA JUICE

SERVES 1

For a desolate desert planet, Tatooine produces a lot of good things: valuable ores, Bantha milk, Skywalkers . . . Another fantastic Tatooine export is Jawa Juice, also known as Ardees. I know the nickname, Jawa Juice, is somewhat alarming; the good news is that Ardees is made *by* Jawas, not *from* Jawas. The bad news is that it *is* made from mashed Bantha hides and fermented grains. The latter isn't so bad—fermented grains are the basis of many great things, like beer! However, Bantha hides are, well, perhaps not the most appetizing ingredient. If I had to imagine a taste, I would say they would taste smoky. This tasty draught combines two kinds of fermented grain alcohols, some citrus, Peychaud's Bitters, and Spiced Maple Syrup, with a finish of bacon-infused ale for the . . . uh . . . protein.

INGREDIENTS

2 fl oz (60 ml) rye whiskey
3–4 teaspoons Spiced Maple
  Syrup (page 16), or to taste
½ fl oz (15 ml) fresh lemon juice
2–3 dashes Peychaud's Bitters
2–3 ice cubes
3 fl oz (90 ml) chilled bacon ale

1. Shake the whiskey, syrup, lemon juice, and bitters in a cocktail shaker with the ice cubes.

2. Pour into a serving glass.

3. Top with the bacon ale.

SUGGESTED GARNISH

The Salted Rim (page 17) with bacon salt

VIRGINIZE

Use nonalcoholic spiced apple cider in place of the whiskey. Reduce the syrup quantity and use ginger ale and a dash of liquid smoke in place of the bacon ale.

TATOOINE SUNSET

SERVES 1

The *Star Wars* cantina is iconic—especially Chalmun's Cantina on Mos Eisley, that wretched hive of scum and villainy. You probably have the music in your head right now. It's understandable: This cantina is where you first saw some of the more colorful aliens that occupy that galaxy far, far away. It's where Obi-Wan unleashed the Force on that ruffian's arm. It's where Han shot first. In the movies, the drinks enjoyed at the cantina are mostly a mystery, but the companion materials, like *Star Wars: Absolutely Everything You Need to Know*, elaborates on them. Among the top five drinks served at Chalmun's is the Tatooine Sunset. This interpretation looks like a sunset with a bright Bantha-blue top and uses spirits developed from desert plants like agave (tequila) and pomegranate.

INGREDIENTS

1½ fl oz (45 ml) silver tequila
½ fl oz (15 ml) blue curaçao
1 fl oz (30 ml) pomegranate
   liqueur
½ fl oz (15 ml) Grenadine
   (page 13)
Cracked ice
½–1 fl oz (15–30 ml) fresh
   lemon juice
2–3 fl oz (60–90 ml) orange
   juice
2 cherries

1. In a small mixing glass, stir together the tequila and blue curaçao. Set aside.

2. In the serving glass, add the pomegranate liqueur and grenadine. Then fill the glass with cracked ice.

3. Add the lemon and orange juices to the serving glass.

4. Carefully pour the tequila and blue curaçao mixture over the back of a spoon so it slowly pours on top of the orange juice.

5. Garnish with the cherries and serve immediately!

SUGGESTED GARNISH

Skewer (page 19) with 2 cherries (to represent both of Tatooine's suns)

VIRGINIZE

Replace the blue curaçao with blue curaçao syrup. Replace the tequila with white grape juice. Replace the pomegranate liqueur with pomegranate juice.

PAN GALACTIC GARGLE BLASTER

SERVES 1

The Hitchhiker's Guide to the Galaxy, by Douglas Adams, is one of the most beloved sci-fi comedies of all time. As such, no fictional cocktail compendium would be complete without the most famous cocktail in the universe: the Pan Galactic Gargle Blaster. Considered by the *Guide* to be the best drink in existence, the effects are described as, well . . . it involves the bludgeoning of one's brains with a lemon-wrapped gold brick. Never drink more than two, if you know where your towel is.

INGREDIENTS

1 sugar cube (Algolian Suntiger tooth)

2 dashes lemon or grapefruit bitters (Zamphuor)

3 fl oz (90 ml) tonic water (Santragian seawater), divided

½ fl oz (15 ml) fresh lemon juice

1 fl oz (30 ml) moonshine (Ol' Janx Spirit)

2 fl oz (60 ml) London dry gin (Arcturan Mega-gin)

Drop of crème de menthe (Qalactin Hypermint extract)

Small piece dry ice (Fallian marsh gas)

1. Add the sugar cube to a serving glass.

2. Add the bitters and about ½ fl oz (15 ml) of the tonic water.

3. Muddle the sugar cube to dissolve it.

4. Add the lemon juice, moonshine, gin, crème de menthe, and the remaining 2½ fl oz (75 ml) tonic water.

5. Stir the cocktail. Then, using the methods on page 23, add the dry ice.

SUGGESTED SERVING VESSEL

Cocktail glass

SUGGESTED GARNISHES/EFFECT

Olive

The Spiral Citrus Peel (page 21) with lemon or orange

The Mist Effect (page 23)

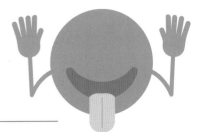

SPICE BEER

SERVES 1-2

Frank Herbert's *Dune* is perhaps the most expansive sci-fi classic where everyone is addicted to drugs. In this world, the Spice Melange is a coveted but highly addictive substance that expands the awareness of the imbiber, which is necessary for interstellar travel. The taste and smell of this spice is described as similar to cinnamon, although more bitter. Melange can be mixed into both food and beverages as an enhancement, which is where Spice Beer comes in. This delicious beer cocktail combines the taste of cinnamon with lemon juice and spicy bitters. The spice beer must flow!

INGREDIENTS

1½ fl oz (45 ml) cinnamon
   liqueur
1½ fl oz (45 ml) bourbon
1 teaspoon fresh lemon juice
2-3 dashes Peychaud's Bitters
2-3 teaspoons Cinnamon Syrup
   (page 15), or to taste
3-4 fl oz (90-120 ml) chilled
   IPA beer

1. In the serving glass(es), stir together the cinnamon liqueur, bourbon, lemon juice, bitters, and syrup.

2. Top with beer and give it one last quick stir.

CULTY
COCKTAILS

SONIC SCREWDRIVER

SERVES 1

Okay, this one is not in the series canon, but the pun is just too good to pass up. The Doctor always carries a Sonic Screwdriver, a handy device with multiple uses that change to suit each of the Doctor's regenerations. In bartending, a "screwdriver" is vodka and orange juice, as many of you know. This version of a screwdriver uses blue curaçao, a blue, orange-flavored liqueur that makes the drink a nice Tardis blue.

INGREDIENTS

2 fl oz (60 ml) vodka
1 fl oz (30 ml) blue curaçao
2 teaspoons fresh lemon juice
1–3 teaspoons Classic Simple
   Syrup (page 11), or to taste
Ice cubes
3–4 fl oz (90–120 ml) orange-
   flavored sparkling water, or
   to taste

1. In a serving glass, stir together the vodka, blue curaçao, lemon juice, and simple syrup.
2. Add ice to the glass and top with the sparkling water.

SUGGESTED SERVING VESSEL

Cocktail glass

SUGGESTED GARNISHES

The Sparkly Rim (page 18) in blue

Edible star sprinkles

EMERGENCY PROTOCOL 417

SERVES 1

This drink appeared in season 2 of the rebooted series, in "The Doctor Dances," an episode featuring gas masks, "Moonlight Serenade," and a banana. Captain Jack Harkness—companion of the Ninth and Tenth Doctors, central character in the popular *Torchwood* spin-off, conman, and all-around fashionable guy—has to carry a bomb away from Earth that would destroy London. A couple of minutes from annihilation, he asks his computer to initiate "Emergency Protocol 417," which turns out to be a martini—a martini that's just a bit heavy on the vermouth. So, now you know what to do if you have only a few minutes left to live!

INGREDIENTS

Ice cubes
1½ fl oz (45 ml) chilled gin
1½ fl oz (45 ml) dry vermouth
1 Spanish olive

1. Chill a coupe or martini glass in the fridge.

2. Add ice to a mixing glass, then pour in the gin and vermouth.

3. Stir for about 30 seconds.

4. Strain into your serving vessel.

5. Skewer the olive with a toothpick and add to the drink.

6. Reminisce about your former executioners.

SUGGESTED SERVING VESSELS

Coupe

Martini glass

WHITE RUSSIAN

SERVES 1 DUDE

The Coen brothers sure do have a knack for making cult films, but the one that has resonated the most is probably the tale of The Dude. There are three things to know about The Dude: he bowls, he chills, and he drinks White Russians. This is a classic White Russian, just the way The Dude likes it. Don't worry, it'll really tie the room together.

INGREDIENTS

Cracked ice
2 fl oz (60 ml) vodka
1½ fl oz (45 ml) coffee liqueur
1½ fl oz (45 ml) half-and-half

1. Add cracked ice to a rocks glass.
2. Pour in the vodka, followed by the coffee liqueur.
3. Top with the half-and-half.
4. Stir.

SUGGESTED DRINKING ATTIRE

Bathrobe

Flip-flops

BLACK YUKON SUCKER PUNCH

SERVES 1–2

This drink is almost as much of a mystery as *Twin Peaks* itself. Appearing in the episode "The Orchid's Curse," Judge Sternwood orders the beverage for Agent Cooper and Sheriff Truman while they discuss the trial of Leo Johnson. The drink appears to be black liquid topped with a light blue foam. The taste is not described, but Judge Sherwood tells Cooper and Truman that the drink will "sneak up on you." This interpretation features the two most important *Twin Peaks* food groups: black coffee and cherry. It's sweetened with Spiced Maple Syrup because nothing beats the taste sensation when maple syrup collides with . . . spices. To complete the cocktail, create a couple peaks in that mysterious blue foam. If Coop drank alcohol, he'd say, "That's a damn fine cup of booze!"

INGREDIENTS

1 fl oz (30 ml) bourbon
1 fl oz (30 ml) Yukon Jack or
   other honey liqueur
1 fl oz (30 ml) cherry liqueur
3 fl oz (90 ml) chilled bold
   coffee
4 teaspoons Spiced Maple
   Syrup (page 16), or to taste,
   divided
3 ice cubes
5 egg whites
2 fl oz (60 ml) blue curaçao
½ tablespoon (8 ml) fresh
   lemon juice
1 teaspoon cream of tartar

1. Add the bourbon, liqueurs, coffee, and 2 teaspoons of the syrup to a cocktail shaker, along with the ice cubes. Shake well.

2. Strain into a highball glass.

3. Add the egg whites (see below for an egg white substitute), blue curaçao, lemon juice, cream of tartar, and the remaining 2 teaspoons syrup to a mixing bowl and whip until (twin) peaks form.

4. Gently spoon the blue foam on top of the black liquid and smooth out the top of it.

EGG WHITE SUBSTITUTE

The egg whites are "cooked" through the foaming process, but some folks may (understandably!) feel icky about using them. If you're one of those, skip steps 3 and 4 and do this instead:

8 fl oz (240 ml) heavy whipping cream
1½ fl oz (45 ml) blue curaçao

3. In a mixing bowl, whip the cream with the blue curaçao and the remaining 2 teaspoons syrup.

4. Spoon the whipped cream mixture on top of the black liquid and smooth it out.

THREE-TOED SLOTH

SERVES 1

It was hard to pick one of the crazy made-up drinks peppered in with the real-life cocktails in Tom Cruise's "Last Barman Poet" poem. There are many to choose from: The Death Spasm? The Dingaling? Honestly, I think we're all the scandalized lady in the audience incredulously asking, "Dingaling?!" But punning is my specialty, so I went with the Three-Toed Sloth. This cocktail uses sloe gin (get it?), with layers approximately the same colors as those of a three-toed sloth and topped with three coffee beans to act as the "toes."

INGREDIENTS

1 fl oz (30 ml) sloe gin
1 fl oz (30 ml) cognac
1 fl oz (30 ml) crème de cacao
2 dashes chocolate bitters
2–3 ice cubes
1 fl oz (30 ml) heavy cream or coconut cream
3 coffee beans, for topping

1. In a cocktail shaker, combine the gin, cognac, crème de cacao, Kahlúa, bitters, and ice cubes.

2. Pour the contents of the cocktail shaker into the serving glass.

3. Pour one-third of the heavy cream out of the carton and set it aside (you can pour it back in later). Vigorously shake the heavy cream carton for about 30 seconds.

4. Hold a spoon upside down over the drink, pointed slightly downward. Slowly pour the cream onto the back of the spoon so that it indirectly spills over the rest of the drink, creating a separate layer.

5. Top with the coffee beans.

SUGGESTED SERVING VESSELS

Pousse-café glass

Martini glass

PURPLE NURPLE

SERVES 3–4

Supernatural is a fantasy-horror series, created by Eric Kripke, that follows brothers Sam and Dean Winchester as they hunt down dangerous supernatural creatures. Hunting is thirsty work, and although they do tend to drink mostly whiskey and beer, the brothers have been known to indulge in the occasional cocktail. Appearing in the season 2 episode "Tall Tales," Dean drinks this concoction while "interrogating" a local grad student at the campus bar. Presumably named Purple Nurple after the horrifying prank that involves twisting, well, you can guess . . . this purple shooter is surprisingly delicious. You really should try it.

INGREDIENTS

3 fl oz (90 ml) coconut rum
1 fl oz (30 ml) blue curaçao
1 fl oz (30 ml) Triple Sec
½ fl oz (15 ml) Grenadine (page 13), or to taste

1. In a mixing glass, stir together the rum, blue curaçao, Triple Sec, and grenadine.
2. Pour the contents of the mixing glass into 3–4 shot glasses.

SUGGESTED SERVING VESSEL

Shot glass

ORANGE WHIP

SERVES 3

The Blues Brothers is a 1980 American musical comedy based on a classic sketch from *Saturday Night Live*. One of the most quoted scenes in a movie filled with quotable material is the "Orange Whip" scene. Orange Whips were a brand of orange soda that served as the primary refreshment for the crew during filming. A crewmember, who had a relative working at the Orange Whip Corporation, asked the director if Orange Whip could be mentioned in the film. The famous scene was then completely improvised by John Candy. This cocktail combines whipped cream vodka and orange soda for a cocktail that will make you see the light! There are 106 miles to Chicago . . .

INGREDIENTS

6 fl oz (180 ml) whipped cream vodka
1½ fl oz (45 ml) spiced rum
1½ fl oz (45 ml) Triple Sec
4–5 ice cubes
9 fl oz (270 ml) orange soda

1. In a mixing glass, stir together the vodka, rum, Triple Sec, and ice cubes.
2. Pour the contents of the mixing glass into three serving glasses.
3. Top each with 3 ounces (90 ml) of the orange soda.

SUGGESTED SERVING VESSEL

Cocktail glass

BLOOD

SERVES 1–2

Ah, blood, the beverage of choice for vampires everywhere. I've said it before: Whether your favorite vampires are tortured souls, sparkly teenagers, ruthless killers, or werewolf-hating roommates in New Zealand, one thing they all have in common is their need for blood. Although there are some outliers in the vampire meta, blood generally has an addictive and intoxicating effect on vampires, much like alcohol has on mortals. This blood recipe contains cherries, along with two mortal vices—coffee and chocolate—to simulate what drinking blood might feel like to a vampire.

INGREDIENTS

½ cup (75 g) frozen pitted
  cherries
2 fl oz (60 ml) white rum
1 fl oz (30 ml) coffee liqueur
Dash chocolate sauce
Dash Grenadine (page 13)
Ice (optional)
3 fl oz (90 ml) tart cherry juice

1. Add all the ingredients to a blender.
2. Blend on the lowest setting until smooth.
3. Let settle before serving.

SUGGESTED SERVING VESSEL

Goblet

SUGGESTED EFFECTS

The Candy Rim (page 19) in red

The Mist Effect (page 23)

VIRGINIZE

Replace rum with 1 fl oz (30 ml) of water. To replace the coffee liqueur, mix 1 fl oz (30 ml) of coffee with 7 teaspoons of sugar.

VESPER

SERVES 1

We all know the James Bond drink order, just like we all think it's really suave to say our last name, then our first name, then our last name again. It may surprise some of the film fans to learn that the shaken vodka martini wasn't always 007's signature drink. The original Bond novel *Casino Royale* (1953), written by Ian Fleming, mentions his first drink order as an Americano, a classic cocktail using equal parts Campari, sweet vermouth, and soda water. Bond's first martini order occurs later in the book. This special martini, called the Vesper after Bond girl Vesper Lynd, coincides with the birth of the "shaken, not stirred" catchphrase. The ingredients and ratios are given in the book, but since Kina Lillet is sadly discontinued, we have a modern substitution in this recipe.

INGREDIENTS

3 fl oz (90 ml) Gordon's gin
1 fl oz (30 ml) vodka
½ fl oz (15 ml) Lillet Blanc or
    Cocchi Americano
2–3 ice cubes

1. Put all the ingredients in a cocktail shaker and shake until ice cold, about 20 seconds.

2. Pour into a serving vessel.

SUGGESTED SERVING VESSEL

Deep champagne goblet

SUGGESTED GARNISH

The Spiral Citrus Peel (page 21) with lemon

SINGAPORE SLING

SERVES 1

The Singapore Sling is a classic cocktail, developed around 1915 by Ngiam Tong Boon, a bartender in Singapore. Perhaps the most notable reference to the drink is in Hunter S. Thompson's *Fear and Loathing in Las Vegas*. The main character, Duke, and his attorney are drinking Singapore Slings by the pool before receiving a catalytic call from Duke's editor. This is a fairly classic Singapore Sling, because, as Duke says, anything worth doing is worth doing right.

INGREDIENTS

Cracked ice and ice cubes
1½ fl oz (45 ml) gin
1 fl oz (30 ml) cherry brandy
½ fl oz (15 ml) Bénédictine
½ fl oz (15 ml) Triple Sec
3 fl oz (90 ml) pineapple juice
2 teaspoons Grenadine
  (page 13), or to taste
Squeeze of fresh lime juice
Dash orange bitters

1. Fill a serving glass with cracked ice.

2. Add all the liquid ingredients to a cocktail shaker with a couple of ice cubes. Shake well.

3. Strain the contents of the shaker into a serving vessel.

SUGGESTED SERVING VESSELS

Collins glass

Hurricane glass

SUGGESTED GARNISHES

Maraschino cherry

Pineapple slice

Cocktail umbrella

Sword skewer (page 19)

TIP

Serve with a side of Mezcal and chase with beer!

BLACK FROST BEER

For some reason, "Beer Bad" seems to rate as one of the worst episodes of *Buffy the Vampire Slayer* in almost every ranking I've ever seen. I don't get it: Cave Buffy is the absolute best! In the episode, a bartender has been spiking Black Frost (one of the brews on tap at UC Sunnydale's campus pub) with a magic concoction that reverts drinkers into literal cavemen. The alchemic setup to make the beer is briefly shown. In it, acid is clearly labeled, but much of the bubbling mystery liquids seem to be distilled into a pale green serum that looks an awful lot like absinthe. Based on the name, I would guess Black Frost is a lager, because lager matures in cold storage. This is a refreshing, foamy beer cocktail that features absinthe, which will make most people act like Neanderthals in any case.

INGREDIENTS

1 fl oz (30 ml) absinthe
1–2 teaspoons Ginger Syrup
  (page 14), or to taste
2–3 dashes grapefruit bitters
Squeeze of fresh lime juice
3–4 fl oz (90–120 ml) chilled
  light lager

1. Add the absinthe, syrup, bitters, and lime juice to a beer glass and stir.
2. Top off with a quick pour of the beer to make it foamier, just how Cave-Buffy likes it.

VIRGINIZE

Use apple cider instead of beer. Omit the absinthe or replace it with anise syrup.

LITERARY
LIBATIONS

BUTTERBEER

SERVES 3-4

The *Harry Potter* series by J. K. Rowling is the bestselling fantasy series of all time, so it comes as no surprise that Butterbeer is one of fiction's most renowned alcoholic beverages. You can actually get an official version at The Wizarding World of Harry Potter at Universal Studios, but if you're like me, you'll want to enjoy it between visits. The alcoholic content of Butterbeer is supposed to be negligible—only containing enough alcohol to get a house elf drunk—so presumably an adult human would have to drink an awful lot of it to get any sort of buzz. Or an adult human could just spike it with some rum!

INGREDIENTS

3 cups (700 ml) stout beer
2 cinnamon sticks
8 whole cloves
8 whole allspice
½ fl oz (15 ml) imitation butter
½ fl oz (15 ml) melted butter
½ fl oz (15 ml) vanilla extract
¼ cup (60 g) brown sugar
2 fl oz (60 ml) evaporated milk
1 fl oz (30 ml) sweetened
    condensed milk, or to taste
3-4 fl oz (90-120 ml) spiced rum

1. Pour the beer into a saucepan, along with the cinnamon sticks, cloves, and allspice.

2. Bring to a boil over high heat, then reduce the heat to medium-low and simmer for about 15 minutes.

3. Remove the spices (with a strained or slotted spoon), but reserve the cinnamon sticks for serving.

4. Stir in the remaining ingredients and simmer for another couple minutes.

5. Pour into 3-4 serving vessels.

SUGGESTED SERVING VESSEL

Mug

SUGGESTED GARNISHES

Cinnamon sticks

Whipped cream

Gold sprinkles

VIRGINIZE

Omit the rum and use a dark nonalcoholic beer.

FIREWHISKY

SERVES 1

Most fans think of the mildly alcoholic but still kid-friendly Butterbeer (see page 98) when they recall the magical beverages of the *Harry Potter* series, and with good reason: It sounds delicious and there's "butter" in the name! However, there's a more adult beverage to order at The Three Broomsticks. Firewhisky is referred to in four of the seven *Harry Potter* books, and Harry drinks it himself in *The Deathly Hallows* as a toast to Mad-Eye Moody. The taste is not described, but it burns Harry's throat and leaves him with a warm feeling like courage. It also seems to be a straight liquor, so I've created a simple whiskey cocktail with spicy cinnamon and orange notes.

INGREDIENTS

1 fl oz (30 ml) rye whiskey
½ fl oz (15 ml) Triple Sec
1½ fl oz (45 ml) cinnamon
   whiskey
1–2 teaspoons Cinnamon Syrup
   (page 15)
1–2 dashes orange bitters
3 ice cubes (optional)

1. In a mixing glass, stir together the rye whiskey, Triple Sec, cinnamon whiskey, syrup, and bitters.

2. Pour the mixture into a serving glass with the ice cubes (if using).

3. Enjoy!

SUGGESTED SERVING VESSELS

Glencairn

Lowball glass

SUGGESTED EFFECT

The Citrus Flame (page 26) with orange

OOSQUAI

SERVES 2

The Wheel of Time, written by Robert Jordan, is an expansive series of high-fantasy novels that have earned their elevated ranking among other fantasy best sellers. Oosquai is a potent drink of the Aiel, a desert-dwelling warrior race. Made from *zemai*, which is the Aiel word for "corn," it is described as brown in color and stronger than double-distilled brandy. Conveniently for us, bourbon is also brown and made with mostly corn. Oosquai does seem to be a straight liquor, so here is a simple bourbon cocktail. Sharing Oosquai with someone is supposed to be a great act of friendship between warriors, so this recipe serves two: you and a friend. Dovie'andi se tovya sagain!

INGREDIENTS

4 fl oz (120 ml) bourbon
1 fl oz (30 ml) sweet vermouth
5–6 dashes Angostura Bitters
3–4 ice cubes

1. Fill the mixing glass with all the liquid ingredients, add the ice, and stir gently for 10–15 seconds.
2. Strain into a serving glass.

SUGGESTED GARNISH/EFFECT

The Spiral Citrus Peel (page 21) with orange
The Citrus Flame (page 26) with orange

COUZI

SERVES 4

Demon Cycle, a fantasy-horror series by Peter V. Brett, takes place in a world where demons come every night to terrorize and kill humans. In this world, Couzi is an extremely potent drink made with fermented grains and cinnamon. Because of its potency, it is served in small cups, and its strong cinnamon smell burns the nostrils. Couzi and other grain alcohols are forbidden by the Evejah, a religious text in the world of *Demon Cycle*. I'm not sure which is scarier, the Evejah or the demon attacks. Seriously, how else are you supposed to cope with demon attacks???

INGREDIENTS

3 fl oz (90 ml) strong rye
  whiskey
1 fl oz (30 ml) cinnamon liqueur
3–4 teaspoons Cinnamon
  Syrup (page 15), or to taste
5–6 dashes ground cinnamon
  or Peychaud's Bitters
2–3 teaspoons fresh lemon
  juice
3 ice cubes

1. Add all the liquid ingredients to a mixing glass with the ice cubes and stir.

2. Pour into four shot glasses.

VIOLET WINE

SERVES 1

The Stormlight Archive, an epic fantasy series written by Brandon Sanderson (the author who completed *The Wheel of Time* series after Robert Jordan passed), takes place in a world that is periodically ravaged by violent storms. More importantly, the wines come in multiple colors! Violet wine is the most flavorful and intoxicating of the wines, which also include sapphire, orange, and yellow. This recipe combines rosé with crème de violette for a nic deep-purple wine that will definitely intoxicate you.

INGREDIENTS

1 fl oz (30 ml) crème de violette
½ fl oz (15 ml) raspberry
    liqueur
½ fl oz (15 ml) fresh lemon
    juice
2–3 ice cubes
4 fl oz (120 ml) dry rosé wine

1. Add the liqueurs and juice to a cocktail shaker with the ice cubes.

2. Strain into a serving glass.

3. Top with the rosé and stir.

SUGGESTED EFFECT

The Shimmer Effect (page 22)

MULLED WINE

SERVES 8-10

The *A Song of Ice and Fire* novels and their TV adaption, *Game of Thrones*, have become a phenomenon that's unprecedented for a fantasy series. Mulled wine appears throughout the series many times, as its warmth makes it a favorite of the men of the Night's Watch. Of course, mulled wine is a real thing that is omnipresent in fantasy literature; it's in everything from *The Canterbury Tales* to *The Elder Scrolls*. Originally called Hipprocras, this drink is at least as old as Rome. There are many versions of this delicious rich and spicy beverage across many cultures, both presently and historically, so this recipe is appropriate for any occasion, whether that's a name-day celebration, a (red, purple, or pink) wedding, or just your standard holiday party.

INGREDIENTS

1 orange

1 lemon

2 bottles (750 ml each) red wine

4–6 fl oz (120–180 ml) brandy (optional)

2-inch (5 cm) piece fresh ginger, peeled and thinly sliced

5 cinnamon sticks

5 cloves

2 black peppercorns

5 whole nutmegs, or to taste

8 whole allspice, or to taste

¾ cup (255 g) honey, or to taste

1. Remove the zest from the orange and lemon in strips, using a knife or vegetable peeler. Set aside.

2. Juice the orange and lemon into a Dutch oven or heavy-bottomed pot with a lid. Then pour the wine and brandy (if using) into the pot.

3. Add the orange and lemon zest, ginger, cinnamon sticks, cloves, peppercorns, nutmegs, allspice, and honey into the same pot and stir for a minute or two.

4. Cover the pot and heat over medium heat until the liquid is hot, being careful not to let it boil. Then reduce the heat to low and simmer for an hour, or until the spices are strong enough for your taste.

5. Strain out the spices or remove them with a slotted spoon before serving.

SUGGESTED GARNISHES

Whole spices

The Citrus Peel (page 21) with lemon or orange

SCUMBLE AND FLUFF

SERVES 1-2

Discworld: everyone's favorite world resting upon the shoulders of four giant elephants standing upon a giant turtle that is floating through space. This is the setting of a beloved series of comedic fantasy novels written by the late and great Terry Pratchett. In *Discworld*, Scumble is made from apples and is strong enough to clean silverware, so it's served in very small amounts. When combined with dwarven ale, it creates a cocktail called Fluff. Sometimes, you just need to imbibe vast amounts of alcohol.

INGREDIENTS

Ice cube
1 fl oz (30 ml) applejack brandy
3–4 dashes apple bitters
1–3 teaspoons Spiced Maple
  Syrup (page 16), or to taste
½ fl oz (15 ml) Apple Pie
  Moonshine (optional)
4 oz (120 ml) bitter ale
  (optional)

1. Add the ice to a mixing glass.
2. Pour in the brandy, bitters, syrup, and moonshine (if using). Stir.
3. Pour into a serving vessel(s).
4. If desired, make it Fluff by adding the ale.

SUGGESTED SERVING VESSELS

Thimble

Shot glass

STRAWBERRY CORDIAL

SERVES 2-4

Redwall is a beloved series of children's fantasy novels written by Brian Jacques. The books are chock-full of mouthwatering food and drink, so it's no wonder the series has its very own official cookbook written by Jacques himself. Strawberry Cordial, also called Strawberry Fizz, is mentioned in almost every book and enjoyed at almost every celebration or feast. It's mainly described as bubbly, cold, and sweet. A cordial can be alcoholic or not; considering this cordial's popularity with the Dibbuns, it may not be alcoholic or it might be only slightly alcoholic. For our purposes, we'll booze it up a bit.

INGREDIENTS

¾ cup (150 g) granulated sugar
1½ cups (350 ml) water
2 pints (700 g) ripe
  strawberries
4 fl oz (120 ml) white rum
1 bottle (750 ml) chilled
  prosecco

1. In a medium saucepan, heat the sugar, water, and strawberries over medium heat until the liquid comes to a boil, stirring occasionally.

2. Once boiling, reduce the heat to a simmer and continue to simmer for 20 minutes, or until the strawberries are tender.

3. Remove the strawberry mixture from the heat and transfer to a blender. Blend until smooth.

4. Place a fine-mesh strainer over a large pitcher and pour the mixture through it. Discard what's in the strainer (or use it for something else).

5. Add your rum to the pitcher, followed by the prosecco. Give it a gentle stir until just blended before pouring into serving glasses.

SUGGESTED SERVING VESSEL

Cordial glass

SUGGESTED GARNISHES

Fresh strawberry slices
Ice with strawberry slices (page 20)

VIRGINIZE

Omit the rum, increase the sugar to 1 cup (200 g), and replace the prosecco with seltzer water.

DYSTOPIAN
POTIONS

VICTORY GIN

SERVES 1

George Orwell's classic 1949 novel, *1984*, was doing dystopia way before it was cool. It takes place in Oceania, a terrifying version of England, where residents are living under an oppressive political regime that watches their every move, and Victory is the only available brand of cigarettes and alcohol. Unsurprisingly, the taste of Victory gin is about as good as you would imagine oppressive government-issued liquor would be. According to Winston, the main character, it smells sickly sweet, like rice wine, and burns like nitric acid. Ah, the taste of conformity . . . Remember, proles: Big Brother is watching you drink.

INGREDIENTS

1 fl oz (30 ml) dry gin
Dash dry vermouth
Dash mirin
Squeeze of fresh lemon juice
Dash Angostura Bitters
2–3 ice cubes

1. Add all the liquid ingredients to a cocktail shaker with the ice cubes. Shake well.
2. Pour into a serving glass.

MOLOKO PLUS

SERVES 1–2

A *Clockwork Orange* is a 1962 dystopian novel by Anthony Burgess featuring a subculture of extremely violent youth gangs in near-future England. The disturbing film adaptation by Stanley Kubrick brought the story to the mainstream. Moloko Plus, also known as Knifey Moloko and Milk-Plus, is a special milk sold to minors at bars. Yes, Moloko Plus is laced with drugs. If you want to make a drug milkshake to peet while resting your nogas on your nagoy dama coffee table with your droogs, that's totally horrorshow. However, I propose that you make this instead. Drink while listening to some Ludwig Van; it'll make you have a warm vibratey feeling all through your guttiwuts.

INGREDIENTS

3 fl oz (90 ml) orange juice (freshly squeezed or unpasteurized)
2 fl oz (60 ml) half-and-half
1 fl oz (30 ml) vanilla vodka
1 fl oz (30 ml) white rum
½ fl oz (15 ml) Triple Sec
1 cup (140 g) crushed ice

1. Blend all the liquid ingredients in a blender with the crushed ice.

2. Pour into a serving glass(es).

SUGGESTED GARNISHES

The Spiral Citrus Peel (page 21) with orange

Orange slice

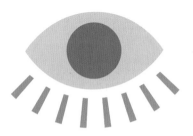

ATOMIC COCKTAIL

SERVES 1

Fallout, a dystopian game series developed by Bethesda Studios, takes place in an alternative retrofuturistic USA after a devastating nuclear war. The Atomic Cocktail appears in *Fallout: New Vegas*, one of the most beloved games in the series. You craft this drink using Nuka-Cola Victory, vodka, and Mentats, which are red, highly addictive stimulants, whose name is a reference to the Mentats of *Dune*, with their superhuman awareness and very red lips. Nuka-Cola Victory radiates a unique orangey color, but the flavor is a mystery. My interpretation features Red Bull (for both its stimulating effect and its color), pineapple soda, and a vodka bomb shot.

INGREDIENTS

2 fl oz (60 ml) chilled pineapple soda
1 fl oz (30 ml) chilled Red Bull
2–3 teaspoons Grenadine (page 13), or to taste
1 fl oz (30 ml) fresh lime juice
2 fl oz (60 ml) vodka

1. Add the soda and Red Bull to a serving glass. Give it a quick stir.

2. Stir in the grenadine and lime juice.

3. Pour the vodka into a shot glass, then drop it into the cola mixture and drink. Kaboom!

SUGGESTED SERVING VESSEL

Highball glass

SUGGESTED EFFECT

The Mist Effect (page 23)

NUKA-COLA DARK

SERVES 1–2

The Nuka-World DLC is the sixth and final add-on to *Fallout 4*, essentially serving as the game's ending. In it, you explore the now-defunct Nuka-World, a theme park owned by the Nuka-Cola company. Many new flavors of sodas are introduced, from Nuka-Berry to Nuka-Cide, but we're focusing on the boozy one. Nuka-Cola Dark is an alcoholic version of Nuka-Cola (see page 146), darker in color and containing a whopping 35% alcohol. The loading screen hints for Nuka-World tell you that the drink was touted as "the most refreshing way to unwind."

INGREDIENTS

Ice cubes
1 fl oz (30 ml) black vodka
1 fl oz (30 ml) spiced rum
1 fl oz (30 ml) raspberry liqueur
4–5 dashes chocolate bitters
3–4 fl oz (60–90 ml) chilled cola

1. Fill a mixing glass with ice cubes.

2. Add the vodka, rum, raspberry liqueur, and bitters. Stir.

3. Strain into a serving vessel(s) and top with cola.

SUGGESTED SERVING VESSEL

Glass soda bottle

CAUTION

Do not operate motor vehicles or heavy machinery for at least 8 hours after drinking.

DIRTY WASTELANDER

SERVES 1-2

Fallout is such an immersive game that it's easy to lose yourself exploring. There's so much freedom and you can do big, important things, like save people, or you can just wander around scavenging for bottle caps and bug meat.

Since the setting is an atompunk wasteland, most of the food is processed, irradiated, and, frankly, not very appetizing. Luckily for us, the cooking system got a very nice revamp in the fourth installment, and there were slightly more appealing recipes for consumables introduced. One of these is the Dirty Wastelander, a cocktail consisting of mutfruit, Nuka-Cola (see page 146), and whiskey. The mutfruit has the appearance of a blackberry/blueberry hybrid, both of which pair excellently with whiskey and cola.

INGREDIENTS

5 blackberries
8 blueberries
1 teaspoon Simple Syrup
  (page 11)
1 teaspoon lemon juice
Ice cubes
2–3 fl oz (60 to 90 ml) whiskey
1¼ cups (300 ml) chilled cola

1. In a serving vessel(s), muddle the blackberries, blueberries, simple syrup, and lemon juice using a muddler or a wooden spoon.

2. Add the ice cubes to the glass.

3. Pour the whiskey into the seving vessel(s), top with the cola, and give the drink a stir before serving.

TIP

To muddle the berries, gently press them against the bottom of the glass with your muddler or wooden spoon, while twisting your wrist for ten to fifteen seconds. Do this until most of the berries' flesh is crushed and you have released some juice.

SOULSTORM BREW

SERVES 1-2

Oddworld, created by developer Oddworld Inhabitants Inc., is a series of games that take place in a fictional world that has been ravaged by industrialization. SoulStorm Brew is a highly addictive drink made by the Glukkons, a greedy race of creatures who have enslaved many of the other races and are forcing them to work in their factories. Indeed, SoulStorm Brew is how they keep the other creatures, especially the Mudokons, under their thumb. As Abe, the main character, discovers, SoulStorm Brew is made from Mudokon bones and tears. This tart, sweet cocktail is unnaturally green and uses gelatin for the Mudokon bones and sea salt for the tears. If you drink too much, seek out the Three Weirdos

INGREDIENTS

½ tablespoon (8 ml) lime
  Jell-O mix
2 fl oz (60 ml) hot water
3 ice cubes
2½ fl oz (75 ml) light rum
½ fl oz (15 ml) melon liqueur
Pinch sea salt
2 fl oz (60 ml) lemon-lime soda

1. In a bowl, dissolve the gelatin in the hot water, stirring for a couple minutes.

2. Add the ice cubes, along with the rum, melon liqueur, and sea salt.

3. Pour into the serving glasses and top with the lemon-lime soda.

COMEDIC
CONCOCTIONS

PEPPERMINT PATTY

SERVES 3–4

Archer is an animated adult sitcom, created by Adam Reed, that follows Sterling Archer, a promiscuous, egotistical secret agent, and his dysfunctional colleagues. We all wish we had Archer's talent for having a drink for every occasion, whether that occasion is a ski trip, a totally ninja-assassination-extrajudicial killing, or both. In the season 6 episode "The Archer Sanction," as Archer, Lana, and Ray are driving to their target in the Alps, Archer pulls out his thermos and gushes about how delicious his creamy concoction is, repeatedly asking Lana to try it. (LANA!!!) Following Archer's recipe pretty much verbatim, this tasty beverage will keep you warm in the Danger Zone!

INGREDIENTS

2 cups (475 ml) prepared
   hot cocoa
1 teaspoon vanilla extract
2 fl oz (60 ml) half-and-half
3½ fl oz (105 ml) dark crème
   de cacao
1 fl oz (30 ml) crème de menthe
3½ fl oz (105 ml) peppermint
   schnapps

1. Remove the hot cocoa from the heat and add the vanilla, half-and-half, crème de cacao, crème de menthe, and peppermint schnapps.

2. Pour into the serving vessels.

SUGGESTED SERVING VESSELS

Thermos

Mug

SUGGESTED GARNISHES

Whipped cream

Cinnamon sticks

Candy canes

6 GUMMY BEARS AND SOME SCOTCH

SERVES 2

Archer can make a cocktail out of pretty much anything, right? He's like the MacGyver of cocktails. I'm not sure I can really call this one a cocktail, but by god, I'm going to try. This is a reference to the first-season episode "Killing Utne," in which all Archer ate was six gummy bears and some Scotch. Oh, and Malory hatches a dinner party assassination scheme that goes awry, but what else is new?

INGREDIENTS

12 Haribo gummy bears
4 fl oz (120 ml) Scotch whisky, plus more for soaking

1. Add the gummy bears to a glass or small bowl. Pour in just enough Scotch whisky to cover them. Let them soak for at least 15 hours.

2. The gummy bears should be big and squishy now, having soaked up all or most of the alcohol. If there's a little alcohol left, that's fine—you can add it to the drink, or you can continue the soak until it's completely absorbed.

3. Split the gummies between two glasses. Pour 2 fl oz (60 ml) of the Scotch into each glass.

4. Enjoy the delicious taste of Scotch with the occasional sweet, chewy gummy bear.

TIP

Make sure you cover the Scotch and gummy bears while soaking, unless you want ants. Because that's how you get ants.

SWANKY-PANKY

SERVES 1

I know it's weird to do a *Bob's Burgers* recipe that isn't a burger, but someone else did the burger thing and did it really well. In the episode "Crawl Space," Teddy mentions that his family invented a cocktail called the Swanky-Panky. Teddy manages to say the drink is two parts vermouth before Bob cuts him off. I wanted to know more, Bob! There is a classic cocktail called the Hanky-Panky, which may have been the inspiration. This recipe is a modified version of that, using Peychaud's Bitters as a nod to the Sazerac, the favorite cocktail of *Bob's Burgers* creator Loren Bouchard. This may get you even more buzzed than Margarita Mix!

INGREDIENTS

Ice cube
2 fl oz (60 ml) sweet vermouth
1 fl oz (30 ml) dry gin
2 dashes Peychaud's Bitters
Orange peel

1. Add the ice cube to a mixing glass.

2. Add the vermouth, gin, and bitters to the mixing glass and stir until chilled.

3. Strain the contents of the mixing glass into a serving glass.

4. Twist an orange peel over the surface of the drink to release the oil or use the Citrus Flame method on page 26.

5. Use the peel for garnish.

SUGGESTED SERVING VESSELS

Coupe

Martini glass

SUGGESTED GARNISHES/EFFECT

The Spiral Citrus Peel (page 21) with orange

Edible gold leaf flakes

The Citrus Flame (page 26) with orange

MOSS WINE

SERVES 1

We're getting pretty meta over here, folks: This recipe is from a fake fantasy series within a police sitcom. *Brooklyn Nine-Nine*, created by Dan Goor and Michael Schur, revolves around Brooklyn's 99th Precinct. In the episode "Return to Skyfire," officers Peralta and Terry are investigating a claim by DC Parlov, writer of *The Skyfire Cycle*, a series of fantasy books that Peralta and Terry are both fans of. So, the two fanboys drag Rosa along as they go "undercover" at a fantasy convention. While they're there, they see a booth serving Moss Wine, a drink mentioned in the *Skyfire* series. Terry wonders aloud if it's as gross as the books say it is. Well, Terry, it's not as gross as the books say it is . . . (title of your sex tape!).

INGREDIENTS

8–10 basil leaves
½ fl oz (15 ml) fresh lemon juice
3 fl oz (90 ml) dry white wine
½ fl oz (15 ml) vermouth
1½ fl oz (45 ml) Ginger Syrup
 (page 14), or to taste
1–2 ice cubes

1. In a cocktail shaker, muddle the basil with the lemon juice.

2. Add the remaining ingredients, plus the ice cube(s). Shake well.

3. Strain into a serving vessel.

SUGGESTED SERVING VESSELS

Wine glass

Goblet

SUGGESTED EFFECTS

The Mist Effect (page 23)

The Candy Rim (page 19) in swampy green

FLANDERS' PLANTER'S PUNCH

SERVES 2-3

The Simpsons, created by Matt Groening, is both America's longest-running sitcom and longest-running animated series. As many of you know, the Simpsons have a neighbor called Ned Flanders, a guy who's just so likeable, you can't help but hate him. Or maybe it's the other way around . . . ? Unlike Ned Flanders, I don't have a PhD in Mixology, but I can tell you that Planter's Punch is a real thing, generally made from dark rum, fruit juices, grenadine, and bitters. This is a modified Planter's Punch, Ned Flanders–style, with 4½ ounces (135 ml) of spiced rum and a jigger of bourbon. Let it fill you with a warm sense of well-being and slur your speech!

INGREDIENTS

4½ fl oz (135 ml) spiced rum
1½ fl oz (45 ml) bourbon
½ fl oz (15 ml) crème de cassis
4 fl oz (120 ml) pineapple juice
3 fl oz (90 ml) orange juice
1 fl oz (30 ml) cold water
½ fl oz (15 ml) fresh lime juice
½ fl oz (15 ml) Grenadine (page
   13), or to taste
2 dashes Angostura Bitters
2–3 ice cubes, plus more if
   desired

1. Add all the liquid ingredients to a large mixing glass with the ice cubes and stir until well combined.

2. Open-pour into serving cups. Add more ice if desired.

SUGGESTED SERVING VESSEL

Clear plastic cup

SUGGESTED GARNISH

Cherry

FIGHT MILK

SERVES 1-2

It's Always Sunny in Philadelphia is a black comedy following a group of five degenerates who run a Philadelphia pub, among other ill-conceived ventures. Fight Milk, in all its avian glory, appeared in the season 8 episode "Frank's Back in Business." Charlie, with Mac's help, comes up with the perfect product for Atwater Company to sell: Fight Milk! Marketed as "the first alcoholic dairy-based protein drink for bodyguards, by bodyguards" in the promotional video, the ingredients include milk, vodka, and crow eggs. This version of the unusual beverage combines egg-based protein powder, vanilla vodka, and malted milk to make something not only edible but actually pretty tasty. Fight like a crow! :: crow sounds ::

1. Add all the ingredients to a blender and blend on high until smooth.

2. Pour into a serving vessel.

3. Soar high as a crow!

INGREDIENTS

2½ fl oz (75 ml) vanilla vodka
8 fl oz (240 ml) whole milk
1 tablespoon egg protein powder
3 tablespoons malted milk
  powder
2–3 teaspoons Brown Sugar
  Syrup (page 16), or to taste
½ cup (70 g) crushed or
  cracked ice

SUGGESTED SERVING VESSEL

Old plastic sports drink bottle

BEER MILKSHAKE

SERVES 2-4

Beer is obviously the best milkshake flavor, right? Created by Rob Grant and Doug Naylor, *Red Dwarf* is a British sci-fi comedy TV series that aired from 1988 to 1999, and it has been recently rebooted as *Red Dwarf XII* and *Red Dwarf XIII*. In the original series, Dave Lister is the last living human aboard a mining ship, along with an assortment of unusual companions. He invents the beer milkshake in the episode "Waiting for God" when ordering breakfast from the computer. After requesting chicken vindaloo and a milkshake, the computer asks him what flavor of milkshake he would like, to which he replies, "Erm, beer." Of course, Leopard Lager would be the best beer to use with this, but because it's in limited supply hereabouts, chocolate stout does a fine job pairing with chocolate ice cream. Enjoy with some spicy curry or chicken Marengo!

INGREDIENTS

16 fl oz (475 ml) chocolate stout
2 fl oz (60 ml) crème de cacao
1 pint (473 ml) chocolate
   ice cream
1 fl oz (30 ml) chocolate sauce,
   or to taste, plus more for
   the glasses

1. Pour the stout, crème de cacao, ice cream, and 1 fl oz (30 ml) chocolate sauce into a blender, and blend on low until just mixed, about 30 seconds. Be careful not to over-blend.

2. Drizzle some chocolate sauce along the sides of milkshake glasses, and then pour the ice cream mixture into them.

SUGGESTED GARNISHES

Whipped cream topped with a maraschino cherry

Chocolate sauce

ALASAKAN
POLAR BEAR HEATER

SERVES 1-2

Before there was Eddie Murphy, there was Jerry Lewis. The original *Nutty Professor* was a sci-fi comedy about an awkward nerd who invents a serum that turns him into a suave but diabolical lady-killer called Buddy Love. It's that guy who orders this crazy concoction at the local club, causing the poor bartender a lot of grief. This recipe is the exact cocktail as dictated by Buddy Love. Yes, including the vinegar. Weirdly, the vinegar is what makes the drink. Take this one home and rub it on your chest. Bonus Double-Geek Fun Fact: This concoction was also referenced in the delightfully cheesy 1980s space rom-com musical *Earth Girls Are Easy*.

INGREDIENTS

2 fl oz (60 ml) vodka
1 teaspoon rum
2 dashes orange bitters
1 teaspoon apple cider vinegar
1 fl oz (30 ml) vermouth
1 fl oz (30 ml) gin
1 teaspoon brandy
1 teaspoon Scotch
Ice cubes

1. Pour all the ingredients into a cocktail shaker.
2. Shake it up "real nice."
3. Pour it into a tall glass(es).
4. Drink, and promptly pass out.

SUGGESTED GARNISHES

The Spiral Citrus Peel (page 21) with lemon

The Spiral Citrus Peel (page 21) with orange

Maraschino cherry

WARNING

You might actually turn to stone drinking this. Adding fresh lemon juice and Classic Simple Syrup (page 11) will make that less likely, however.

NONALCOHOLIC
BEVERAGES

BLUE MILK

SERVES 1

Alright, you scruffy-looking nerf herders, this is the most well-known food in the *Star Wars* universe. Otherwise known as Bantha Milk or Tatooine Milk, this is the mysterious beverage that Luke Skywalker and his aunt and uncle are seen drinking at breakfast, right before Luke's adventures begin in *Star Wars Episode IV: A New Hope*. The drink has appeared in countless *Star Wars* games, books, and movies since. I know this recipe sounds a bit strange, but have you seen a Bantha? They look like a cross between a mammoth, a ram, and a garbage truck. I've seen a lot of *Star Wars* fans trying to get their Luke Skywalker on just by adding blue food coloring to their milk. That's great, but I wanted to take it one step further and make this beverage taste like it could actually be milk from a bizarre creature living in a galaxy far, far away. So, the goat milk gives it a sort of unusual quality, and the avocado adds some additional protein and thickness. I think it tastes quite nice. Of course, other milks can be substituted if you're vegan/allergic/grossed out by goats.

INGREDIENTS

8 fl oz (240 ml) goat's
  milk (other milks can be
  substituted)
2 tablespoons avocado
1 fl oz (30 ml) blueberry syrup
1 scoop vanilla ice cream
4–5 drops blue food coloring

1. Use the Force to blend all the ingredients together. Or a blender.

2. Pour into your vessel of choice.

3. Enjoy!

LON LON MILK

SERVES 2

The first 3-D *Zelda* game, *Ocarina of Time* (where Lon Lon Milk made its first appearance), is widely considered to be the best game of all time. Whenever I mention possibly making a recipe for Lon Lon Milk, someone always says, "Isn't it just milk?" Boo! Boo to that. Hyrule is a magical land where Ocarinas have magical powers and, you know, there are fairies and sentient trees and stuff. Did everyone forget that the cows will have a conversation with you if you play them a song? When's the last time you had a discussion with a dairy cow? I don't think the milk in Hyrule would be "just milk." Lon Lon Milk is known among Hylians for being very nutritious. When Link drinks it, it restores five hearts. So, I kept this one simple and healthy, but extremely tasty. There's an apple (or apple sauce) to add a multitude of vitamins, frozen yogurt for a protein boost (which helps restore muscle tissue), and some sweet caramel to keep your spirits up. It tastes like liquid caramel apple and will legitimately boost your immune system.

INGREDIENTS

8 fl oz (240 ml) milk
1 green apple, cored and
roughly chopped, or ½ cup
(122 g) applesauce
2–3 scoops vanilla frozen
yogurt
½ fl oz (15 ml) caramel sauce

1. Blend all the ingredients together in a blender until smooth.

2. Pour into the serving vessels.

3. Drink half of it in one gulp, wipe your mouth, and let out a satisfied sigh.

SUGGESTED SERVING VESSEL

Glass bottle

SLURM

SERVES 1

Futurama is an animated adult comedy TV show created by Matt Groening of *The Simpsons* fame. As the title suggests, the series takes place in the future. The main character, Philip J. Fry, is a present-day pizza delivery guy who becomes cryogenically frozen (by accident) and awakens in the thirty-first century. Though the series is primarily a comedy and can be absurd, it has a strong science-fiction foundation and many geeky references. In addition to appearing in *Futurama*'s opening credits, Slurm is featured prominently in the episodes "Fry and the Slurm Factory" and "The Bots and the Bees." In "Fry and the Slurm Factory" it becomes clear that Slurm is a wildly popular and addictive soft drink. The drink's actual slogan is "It's highly addictive!" The beverage is created on the planet Wormulan, where the *Futurama* crew discover that the primary ingredient is, well, really gross. However, Fry is so addicted that he elects not to reveal the beverage's disgusting origins to the world in fear that Slurm will no longer be manufactured. In "The Bots and the Bees," Fry drinks so much of the newest Slurm drink, Slurm Loco, that he becomes radioactive. It is not specifically stated what Slurm tastes like, so I made my own delicious Slurm ooze by combining frozen limeade with mint jelly and adding soda water for carbonation.

INGREDIENTS

¼ cup (80 g) mint jelly
1½ fl oz (45 ml) frozen limeade
8 fl oz (240 ml) soda water
Green food coloring (optional)
Ice cubes, for serving

1. Blend together the mint jelly and frozen limeade in a blender.

2. Pour the newly made green sludge into the serving vessel.

3. Add the soda water and stir until everything is evenly incorporated. If the drink is too strong for your liking, add more soda water and stir again.

4. Enjoy over ice!

ENT DRAUGHT

SERVES 1

This beverage makes its first appearance in the second book of *The Lord of the Rings* trilogy, *The Two Towers*. As fans will know, the Ents were the ancient tree-people of Middle-earth, dwelling in Fangorn Forest. Merry and Pippin spend a lot of time in the Fangorn Forest after escaping Saruman's clutches, and there they make friends with Treebeard, the eldest of the Ents. During their time in Treebeard's "house," Merry and Pippin are given the drink of the Ents. The draught gives the Hobbits the feeling of being refreshed from the tips of their toes up to the ends of the hair on their heads, and makes Merry and Pippin grow quite a few inches taller than average Hobbit size. The flavor of the drink is supposed to be light, as the drink is described as being like water but has a taste that reminds the Hobbits of the smell of wood from a distance carried by a cool breeze . . . or something like that. For this I used plant-based ingredients with bright earthy/leafy flavors and sweetened the drink with tree sap (maple syrup). Making this invigorating beverage is so quick and simple, you'll be done long before Treebeard can say "Ent Draught."

INGREDIENTS

10 mint leaves
1 fl oz (30 ml) pure maple syrup
1 teaspoon fresh lemon juice
Drop almond extract
8 fl oz (240 ml) chilled lightly
   brewed green tea

1. In a serving glass, muddle the mint leaves in the maple syrup using a muddler or a wooden spoon.

2. Add the lemon juice and almond extract to the muddled mint.

3. Pour the green tea into a serving glass and stir to combine.

NUKA-COLA QUANTUM

SERVES 1–2

Nuka-Cola was invented in 2044 and quickly became the most popular soft drink in the post-apocalyptic world of *Fallout*. It's supposed to contain the essence of seventeen different fruits, which gives it its unique and irresistible flavor. In addition to a super-delicious and nutritious "mild radioactive strontium isotope," Nuka-Cola's second version, Nuka-Cola Quantum, contains an eighteenth fruit essence: pomegranate. It was a bit of a puzzle to figure out how to make a recipe for a glowing radioactive soda with entirely artificial flavoring. Luckily, I like me some puzzles. Hawaiian Punch and Sunny D don't contain anything natural and have a mixture of fruit-like flavors, so I thought these would work pretty well for the base. I made sure to include some pomegranate syrup to make it uniquely Quantum, and the rest is pretty much self-explanatory. Prepare to increase your action points by twenty, and radiation levels by ten!

INGREDIENTS

2 fl oz (60 ml) Hawaiian Punch (Berry Blue or a mix of Berry Blue and Aloha Morning)
2 fl oz (60 ml) Blue Raspberry Sunny D
1½ teaspoons pomegranate syrup or pomegranate molasses
1½ teaspoons vanilla syrup
Caffeine additive (optional), use as package directs
6 fl oz (180 ml) soda water (or tonic water, but it will taste bitter)

SUPPLIES

Glass soda bottle (optional)
Scotch tape (optional)
Nuka-Cola Quantum label (optional)
Small LED light (optional)

1. In a pitcher, stir all the ingredients—except the soda water—together.

2. Add the soda water (or tonic water, which will make the beverage glow under a blacklight) to the mixture and stir.

3. Pour into the soda bottle or other serving vessel of your choice.

4. Tape your printed label to the bottle.

5. To make the soda "glow," tape the small LED light to the bottom of the bottle with the lighted side facing up into the bottle.

MILK OF THE POPPY

SERVES 1-2

Weirdly, this is one of the recipes I get the most requests for, and I've been avoiding it because, well . . . you guys know this is a drug, right? I know it sounds like a fun, soothing beverage but the leading theory is that it's supposed to be laudanum, which is a tincture made from opium, which is made from a certain type of poppy. That's why everyone in the series is less than enthusiastic to drink it, because even though they've just had their face sliced in half, it makes coherent thought difficult, and that's assuming you don't slip into a mini-coma for a few days. You've got to keep your wits about you when you play the game of thrones. However, I'm happy to make a "lite" version. There are a few ingredients which have a similar—although considerably less powerful—effect. Warm milk is a soothing, natural sedative. Turmeric is a very effective natural painkiller, among many other things. Cinnamon and ginger not only taste great, but they also have anti-inflammatory properties. And, even though the honey is mostly there to make this elixir more palatable, it does have some antibiotic properties. I don't recommend this drink for severe injuries, like being gored by a boar, but it will ease milder aches and pains and help you sleep.

INGREDIENTS

16 fl oz (475 ml) milk
1 teaspoon vanilla extract
2 teaspoons turmeric powder
½ teaspoon ground cinnamon
1-2 round slices fresh ginger,
  peeled
Pinch black pepper
Honey, to taste

1. Pour the milk into a saucepan over medium heat. Add the vanilla, turmeric, cinnamon, ginger, and pepper. Stir well as the milk begins to simmer.

2. Let simmer for a minute or two, being mindful that the milk doesn't overheat.

3. Turn off the heat and cover the pan, then leave to infuse for 5-10 minutes.

4. When ready to drink, strain the milk into a serving glass(es), then stir in the honey.

POE-POE

SERVES 2

Most of us '90s kids have a soft spot in our hearts for *Hook*. One of the most memorable scenes in this movie is when Peter, after a long day of being tortured by adolescents, finally sits down to enjoy supper, only to learn that the Lost Boys eat imaginary food instead of real food. Peter hasn't really recovered his imagination by this point, so he watches enviously as the Lost Boys merrily chow down on their make-believe grub. That is until he gets into a very creative insult fight with Rufio and playfully slings some of the imaginary food at him. Suddenly, Peter rediscovers his imagination and can finally see the food. Obviously, an epic food fight ensues . . . because epic food fights are an inevitability in any '90s kids' film. The imaginary smorgasbord in this scene seems to be comprised primarily of colorful whipped cream with some ham hocks and a giant cheese wheel thrown in for fun. However, one Neverfood that is mentioned by name and is briefly shown is Poe-Poe. In the script for *Hook* the food is called Papaw, which is another word for "papaya," but in the film, the captions read "Poe-Poe," and it's depicted as a creamy, frothy drink that leaves a milk mustache on Peter's face when he takes a sip. My take on this frothy Neverdrink will take you back to your childhood, with hints of candy, cake, and bubblegum. *Bangarang.*

INGREDIENTS

16 fl oz (475 ml) whole milk
2 scoops orange sherbet
½ strawberry papaya, peeled, seeded, and cut into rough chunks
½ banana
½ teaspoon ground cinnamon
½ cup (60 g) box cake mix
Rainbow sprinkles, plus more for topping
Whipped cream, for topping

1. Throw all the ingredients—except the sprinkles and whipped cream—into the blender, then blend for about a minute.

2. Add a small fistful of sprinkles and blend again for a second or two.

3. Pour into serving glasses and top with whipped cream and more rainbow sprinkles.

PUMPKIN JUICE

SERVES 2-4

Pumpkin Juice seems to be the Muggle equivalent of our beloved orange juice. Witches and wizards mostly drink it with breakfast, but it can be served with any meal or even enjoyed on its own. Like orange juice, it packs a punch, nutritionally speaking, being rich in fiber, antioxidants, vitamins, and minerals. It will keep you sharp and vibrant for your potions final and properly hydrated for a Quidditch match. You can even use it to slip your friend some liquid confidence, whether that means alcohol or Felix Felicis to you. Wizards can presumably use a spell to extract the juice from the pumpkin, but Muggles will either need a juicer (recommended) or a blender and strainer.

INGREDIENTS

1 small sugar pumpkin, peeled with pulp removed
1 apple, cored, peeled, and sliced
2 carrots, peeled and diced
1-inch (2.5 cm) slice ginger, or to taste, peeled
1 tablespoon (15 ml) ground cinnamon, or to taste
1 teaspoon vanilla extract
1 fl oz (30 ml) Classic Simple Syrup (page 11), or to taste
Ice cubes, for serving (optional)

1. **Using a juicer:** Dice the pumpkin into small chunks.

2. Add the pumpkin, apple, carrots, and ginger to the juicer, and juice the produce into a serving vessel.

3. Combine the cinnamon, vanilla, and simple syrup, then stir that into the juice and serve!

1. **Using a blender and strainer:** Preheat the oven to 350°F (180°C).

2. Cut the pumpkin in half using a serrated knife. Put the pumpkin halves into a clean roasting pan. Cover the pan with foil and roast for about 90 minutes, or until the flesh of the pumpkin is soft and juicy but not burnt. Once cooked, the pan will have juice at the bottom, so reserve that and set it aside.

3. Take some of the pumpkin flesh and wrap it in cheesecloth—you will probably have to do this a little at a time. Over a large bowl, squeeze the flesh through the cheesecloth so that the juice goes into the bowl. Get as much juice as you can—you should get about a 2 cups (475 ml) or more from the whole pumpkin. I also recommend saving the leftover pumpkin pulp as it works great in baked goods and smoothies.

4. Combine the pumpkin juice and all the other ingredients—except the ice—in a blender and blend. It will be frothy, but don't worry, it will eventually settle. Add ice to serve right away or set in the fridge for an hour or so until cool.

KLAH

SERVES 1

Dragonriders of Pern is a series of science-fiction novels written by Anne McCaffrey and occasionally her son, Todd McCaffrey. Pern is the planet on which the series takes place. Periodically, the planet is threatened by Threadfall, which is caused by another rogue planet in the solar system passing close enough to Pern to rain down destructive spores on the planet. The only creatures that can destroy the Thread are genetically engineered sentient dragons that have the ability to teleport through time and space. These dragons come in various sizes and colors and all form a psychic bond with human riders from birth. If you're into dragons and want to see a different take on the mythical creatures, I highly recommend these books. If you're not into dragons, what the hell is wrong with you? Dragons are magnificent! So, Klah is a hot, invigorating, and spicy drink made from tree bark and enjoyed by all of the Pernese. It has a pungent, spicy taste with notes of chocolate and cinnamon. It can be taken with some milk or cream, or even liquor. In the world of Pern, people are as addicted to Klah as we are to coffee. Honestly, I'm surprised they don't have a Starbucks equivalent for Klah lattes and frappuccinos . . . pumpkin spice Klah, decaf iced Klah, nonfat Klah latte with two pumps of caramel, no whip . . . Okay, I'm done.

INGREDIENTS

1 cup (240 ml) brewed coffee (instant or made using a machine)
1 ounce (28 g) bittersweet dark chocolate
Pinch cayenne powder
Pinch allspice
1 cinnamon stick
Splash of cream and/or liquor, for serving (optional)

1. While the coffee is brewing, blast the dark chocolate in a serving glass or mug in the microwave on high for 1 minute.

2. Add the cayenne and allspice to the melted chocolate in the glass.

3. Pour the hot coffee onto the melted chocolate and spices in the glass.

4. Stir everything together with the cinnamon stick.

5. Enjoy plain or with a splash of cream and/or liquor!

RAKTAJINO

SERVES 1:

Raktajino is Klingon coffee. While Raktajino is sometimes enjoyed in other *Star Trek* series, it's no secret that every character in *Deep Space Nine* is hopelessly addicted to it. The first step to recovery is admitting you have a problem, *DS9* crew. Honestly, I would bet that the word "Raktajino" is said more often in *Deep Space Nine* than the words "Deep Space Nine" in tandem. They may as well have named the series *Star Trek: Raktajino*. There are no specifics about how exactly this Klingon coffee differs from Earth coffee, but we can guess that it's probably about twice as strong as a standard human coffee. After all, it's made for Klingons, who are about twice as strong as a standard human. For this recipe I combined the method of Vietnamese coffee with the spices in Moroccan-style coffees.

INGREDIENTS

1 fl oz (30 ml) sweetened condensed milk
1½ fl oz (45 ml) ground (medium-coarse) medium-dark roast coffee with chicory
Pinch ground cardamom
Pinch ground black pepper
Pinch ground nutmeg
Pinch ground ginger
Pinch ground clove
4 fl oz (120 ml) plus 4 teaspoons boiling filtered water, divided
1 Vietnamese coffee filter*

*These can be purchased cheaply at any Asian grocery store or online.

1. Add the sweetened condensed milk to a serving vessel.

2. Add the coffee grounds to the base of a coffee press, then add the spices on top of the grounds. Wet these with the 4 teaspoons of hot water.

3. Screw the press on tight, making sure the coffee is well-packed down. If you don't have the kind that screws, don't worry. Place the filter on top of the mug.

4. Pour the remaining ½ cup (120 ml) boiling water into the coffee press and cover with the lid. Wait for the coffee to drip into the serving vessel until all the water is gone.

5. Remove the filter, stir the coffee into the milk, and enjoy!

INDEX

Cassandra Reeder is an experienced blogger, avid home cook, and lifetime geek. For over a decade she has been helping other geeks all over the world make their fictional food fantasies come true at www.geekychef.com. She is also the author of *The Geeky Chef Strikes Back* and *The Geeky Chef Drinks*. Cassandra currently lives and cooks in Portland, Oregon, with her husband, son, and a magical talking parrot.